Great American
WREATHS

Great American
WREATHS

CREATED BY Martha Stewart and Hannah Milman
DIRECTED BY Gael Towey

PHOTOGRAPHS BY William Abranowicz

No part of this book may be reproduced in any form or by any means without the prior written permission of the publisher.

Originally published in book form by Time Warner in 1996.

Published simultaneously by Clarkson N. Potter, Inc., Oxmoor House, Inc., and Leisure Arts.

A portion of this work was previously published in MARTHA STEWART LIVING.

Manufactured in the United States of America.

Library of Congress Catalog Number: 96-70330

ISBN: 0-8487-1530-6 (hardcover)

0-8487-1531-4 (softcover)

DESIGNER: Laura Harrigan
WRITER: Ingrid Abramovitch
MANAGING EDITOR: Amy Schuler

Contents

ALABAMA
cotton

ALASKA
sitka spruce

ARIZONA
cactus

CONNECTICUT
mountain laurel

DELAWARE
american holly

GLOSSARY OF
Wreaths

FLORIDA
citrus fruits

ILLINOIS
prairie grass

INDIANA
peonies

IOWA
dent corn

KANSAS
sunflowers

MARYLAND
black-eyed susans

MASSACHUSETTS
cranberries

MICHIGAN
woodland

ARKANSAS
rice

CALIFORNIA
olive and rosemary branches

COLORADO
blue spruce

GEORGIA
pecans

HAWAII
orchids

IDAHO
beans

KENTUCKY
bluegrass

LOUISIANA
magnolia

MAINE
eastern white pine

MINNESOTA
red norway pine

MISSISSIPPI
magnolias

MISSOURI
black walnuts

MONTANA
ponderosa pinecones

NEBRASKA
miniature indian corn

NEVADA
tumbleweed

NEW HAMPSHIRE
pussy willow

NEW JERSEY
boxwood

NORTH DAKOTA
oats and barley

OHIO
ohio buckeye

OKLAHOMA
winter wheat

SOUTH DAKOTA
hay

TENNESSEE
galax

TEXAS
yellow roses

VIRGINIA
dogwood

WASHINGTON
moss

WASHINGTON, D.C.
white oak

NEW MEXICO
sagebrush

NEW YORK
rose hips

NORTH CAROLINA
fraser fir

OREGON
apples and pears

PENNSYLVANIA
mountain laurel

RHODE ISLAND
quahaug shells

SOUTH CAROLINA
okra

U.S. TERRITORIES
tropical leaves

UTAH
mixed evergreens

VERMONT
sugar-maple leaves

WEST VIRGINIA
rhododendron

WISCONSIN
wood violets

WYOMING
limber pine

Introduction

THE INSPIRATION FOR THIS BOOK on great American wreaths came to me as I was interviewing First Lady Hillary Rodham Clinton right before Christmas. I was visiting the White House to discuss the amazingly beautiful decorations that adorn it every year. First Ladies have traditionally been very involved with the holiday embellishments, and individuals from all over America contribute ideas, ornaments, and creativity. The idea of a wreath for each state seemed to me an appropriate and wonderful way to celebrate our nation's natural beauty and the extremely diverse resources that distinguish state from state.

I told Mrs. Clinton and her staff about the idea, and they loved it. Hannah Milman, one of MARTHA STEWART LIVING's talented style editors, began the research, and what she uncovered in a year of intense investigative work is depicted in the pages of this book. We started with a list of the fifty states, the territories, and our nation's capital. Then came a list of state trees and flowers, major agricultural products, minerals, and produce. The U.S. Department of Agriculture and its Forest Service, as well as the National Parks Service, state agencies, and universities were consulted. Growers, farmers, gardeners, friends, and myriad others were wonderfully helpful and, in many instances, provided raw materials. Libbie and Bo Dougan sent us rice from their Arkansas rice plantation. Cotton on the branch was sent to us by a grower in Alabama.

To some it seemed as if it would be difficult to invent fifty-two wreaths, but Hannah and I knew that the real problem would be to choose fifty-two out of the hundreds we conceived. The wreath for California, one of the most agriculturally varied states, was especially hard to design. A combination of fresh rosemary and olive boughs, it was inspired both by the state's vegetation and by the fact that California has been one of the most important sources of culinary originality.

History also played a part in determining which materials were used. Our wreath of glistening red cranberries for Massachusetts reminds us that the cranberry is one of the only fruits native to America, and that the state is still the largest producer of this wonderful fruit. The quahaug, a large clam, has been of great import to the tiny seaside state of Rhode Island, and our wreath of its specially cleaned shells is both beautiful and long-lasting.

This book is organized into chapters devoted to different wreath-making methods: Dried materials are applied to wire wreath forms; soil-filled, moss-wrapped forms are the basis for living wreaths; gatherings of prairie grasses, swags of evergreens, and even a giant tumbleweed became wreaths. One of my particular favorites is the bluegrass wreath from Kentucky, a wreath I watered diligently as the grass seed sprouted and grew. I used scissors to even out the length of the blades of green grass, and when the wreath was finally photographed, its romantic beauty took one's breath away. Equally lovely is the dogwood wreath from Virginia, its branched base and dried blossoms coming together in a wreath that is delicate and so versatile—perfect for Christmas or any time of year.

And lastly, the oak-leaf-and-gilded-acorn wreath, which the First Lady and I hung on the iron balustrade of the South Portico of the White House. You'll find instructions for making it on page 139. It is the quintessential wreath—perfect proportions, elegant materials, carefully constructed, exquisitely crafted, and long-lasting. Mrs. Clinton and I both found it exactly right for the place, the time, and the purpose.

Martha Stewart

MISSISSIPPI (Magnolias) The southern magnolia may connote delicacy, but as everyone in the Magnolia State knows, there is nothing fragile about this native evergreen. *Magnolia grandiflora,* the official state tree and flower, grows wild throughout the state, thriving in the basins of the Big Black and Pearl Rivers, and amid the rock outcroppings of Tishomingo County in northeast Mississippi. The elegant and fragrant magnolia is a favorite ornamental tree, found in gardens from Tupelo to Biloxi. Almost every Mississippian has a childhood memory of magnolias: The tree in a grandparent's garden or those lining the paths that led to school. Since 1962, Mississippians have planted *grandiflora* at every major entry point to the state, so that motorists are welcomed by an "Avenue of the Magnolias." We made Mississippi's wreath out of *grandiflora*'s dramatic leaves, which are large and leathery in texture, glossy green on one side, velvety rust brown on the other, and available year-round.

ABOVE: To make the Mississippi wreath, cut 200 branches of *Magnolia grandiflora* into 10"-long sections, and gather into bundles of 5 branches each. Turn some leaves so that the rust-colored backs face out, contrasting with the shiny green surfaces. Attach bundles of leaves to wreath form using the following basic technique.
WIRED-WREATH TECHNIQUE: Attach floral wire on a paddle to the crossbar of a 22" circular wreath form. Lay a leaf bundle on the form and wrap the wire tightly around the stems three times. Do not cut wire. Add another leaf bundle, overlapping previous one by half; wrap wire around stems. Continue adding leaf bundles until you reach the starting point. Tuck wire under form, secure with a knot, and cut. Create a wire hanging loop on the back of the form. Attach a 3-yard-long taffeta ribbon tied in a bow.

OPPOSITE: We used 24 ears of dent corn, but any dried corn will work. The wreath base is a 30" circular double-wire form. Flatten natural raffia ribbon and wrap around frame to cover. Secure floral wire on a paddle to wreath form. Open husks to expose a small section of corn. Wire one ear of corn at a time, wrapping tightly around base of corn to secure. Do not cut wire. Continue adding ears of corn, changing the angle with every other ear. Cut wire and secure. Cover any exposed wire with extra husks using a glue gun.

IOWA (Dent corn) "Io-way, Io-way, that's where the tall corn grows." The "Iowa Corn Song" is the unofficial anthem of this state, which grows an average of 1.7 billion bushels each year, making it the biggest corn producer in the nation. Iowa's rich, deep topsoil provides the perfect growing conditions for corn, the state's largest crop. Corn has always played a part in Iowan culture, from Sioux City's nineteenth-century corn palaces to the corn-husking contests of the 1920s and '30s that were broadcast on national radio. Iowan Henry A. Wallace, a former vice president, developed high-yield hybrid corn in the '30s, which now makes up 80 percent of the nation's corn. Iowa's wreath was made from dent corn, the variety most commonly grown for animal feed. It gets its name from the small dent in the crown of each kernel.

COLORADO (Blue spruce) Amidst
the conifers that grow in the valleys and
foothills of Colorado, blue spruce
(Picea pungens)—the state tree—literally
stands apart. "It's something of an
aloof stranger, living alone or scattered
in small groups intermixed with other
trees," says Dr. Yan Linhart, a tree
biologist at the University of Colorado.
This spruce's solitary existence only
increases its majesty; some grow as
tall as eighty feet. Colorado blue spruce
is best known for the startling silver-
blue color of its needlelike leaves.
The unusual color is produced by a waxy
substance on its foliage and ranges
from steel blue to dark green. This evergreen grows wild in the Rocky Mountains
and has a long history of practical use.
Native Americans collect its needles to
make a tea rich in Vitamin A. Turpentine
is made from the terpenes in its bark.
The shape of the blue spruce, with
branches that graduate from wide at
the bottom to a perfect point at the top,
is the epitome of a Christmas tree.
Those branches hang all the way to the
ground, and Larry Helburg, a forester
with the Colorado State Forest Service,
says the blue spruce has saved many
a traveler's life by providing sanctuary
in a snowstorm.

ABOVE: Because Colorado's wreath was designed to decorate a
barn door, we made it 5' high and wide. But like all the wreaths
in this book, it would be just as attractive on a smaller scale.
Wear work gloves when handling blue spruce or any evergreen,
since the needles are very prickly and the sap can be sticky.

OPPOSITE: Cut 230 branches into 10"-long tips, and group these
into bunches of 6. Secure floral wire on a paddle to the crossbar
of a circular metal wreath form with a double hoop. Lay the first
bunch of spruce on the form. Wrap floral wire around stems three
times to secure. Do not cut the wire. Continue adding bunches
all around wreath form, overlapping each bundle by half. When
finished, secure floral wire with a knot and create a hanging loop
on the back of the frame. To add the pinecones, cut a 20" piece
of floral wire for each cone. Lay a pinecone on its side along center of wire, and twist wire around base of cone three times, leaving ends loose. Attach the pinecones to the wreath in groups of
six, threading wire ends through the branches and knotting it
onto the brackets of the frame. Repeat, placing clusters of cones
in several places on the wreath. Trim excess wire.

COLORADO
BLUE SPRUCE

NEW HAMPSHIRE
PUSSY WILLOW

ABOVE: This Fraser-fir wreath is made on a rectangular wire frame measuring 22" by 23". Cut 140 branches into tips 8" long; gather into bunches of 6 stems. Secure 24-gauge floral wire on a paddle to the frame. Lay first bunch on the form and wrap wire tightly three times around to secure branches to frame. Continue wiring successive branch bundles using the wired-wreath technique described on page 19. Even when dry, Fraser-fir needles will stay on their branches for several months and scent any room where the wreath is hung.

LEFT: The New Hampshire pussy-willow wreath can be made in almost any size. We used a 12" wire-wreath form. Cut 130 fresh pussy-willow branches into 8"-long tips. Secure floral wire on a paddle to the wreath form. Group pussy-willow tips into bunches of 20, arranging the longer tips on the outside of the bunch and the smaller ones on the inside. (This helps create the smooth inner edge of the wreath.) Lay the first bundle on the form and wire tightly. Do not cut wire. Continue adding bundles of pussy willows, overlapping each bunch by half, all around the wreath form. When finished, cut off and secure wire.

BELOW: To cover any holes or exposed wire, create smaller bunches of pussy-willow tips. Wrap brown floral tape around floral wire, secure the bunches, and push them into any gaps.

NORTH CAROLINA (Fraser fir)

Every other year, the National Christmas Tree Association holds a contest to choose the White House Christmas tree. More often than not, a Fraser fir from North Carolina wins. This evergreen, fragrant and lovely with its silver and green foliage, is the only fir native to the southeastern United States. Its popularity as a Christmas tree also comes from its ability to retain its needles. "Put that tree in your house at Thanksgiving, and it will keep its needles way into January," says Patricia Wilkie, executive director of the North Carolina Christmas Tree Association. Fraser fir *(Abies fraseri)* grows wild in the Blue Ridge Mountains of North Carolina, but it has been decimated in recent years by an insect called balsam woolly adelgid and is classified as a federal candidate rare species. "It is regenerating right now, but nobody knows what the effect will be," says Gary Kauffman, a botanist in Nantahala National Forest, in the western part of the state. To protect Fraser firs in the wild, make this wreath from branches obtained from one of North Carolina's many commercial growers.

NEW HAMPSHIRE (Pussy willow)

Pussy willow is beloved in New Hampshire not just because it is soft and fuzzy. This native plant is a harbinger of spring, appearing after the snow has finally melted and the weather is warm enough for the buds to sprout. There are about a dozen species of willow (genus *Salix*) native to New Hampshire that look quite similar to the pussy willow *(Salix discolor)*. The downy parts are called catkins, each a tiny cluster of hundreds of flowers without petals. Pussy willow grows in damp areas such as open meadows. It buds in March or April for a few weeks until its catkins fall off. Then the stamens start poking through and the willows begin to shed their pollen. The best time to pick pussy willow is in the catkin stage. If you cut it and keep the branches dry, they will last for at least several months. Most land in New Hampshire is privately owned, so you must obtain the permission of the landowner to pick pussy willow. In public areas, you don't need special permission, as it's not an endangered species. Pussy willow can also easily be found at any florist.

WYOMING (Limber pine) It's a loner tree with a lot of character, surviving on windblown rocky terrain where few other trees would even think to grow. No wonder the people of Wyoming are fond of their limber pine: In some ways, this conifer is a metaphor for their own rugged temperament. The Latin name for this western tree is *Pinus flexilis,* meaning "flexible" or "limber." "You can literally tie the branches like a pretzel," says Walt Fertig, a botanist with the Nature Conservancy in Laramie, Wyoming. That makes limber pine an excellent candidate for wreath-making, although Fertig warns that fresh branches will be sticky from sap, so he recommends wearing sturdy gloves when working with the branches. Eventually the branches dry out, and the wait is worth it, since limber pine's needle clusters are a beautiful sage green. The best place to find this Wyoming native is in lower elevations in mountainous regions such as Yellow-stone and the Grand Tetons. There is no formal protection of limber pine in Wyoming, since it is not an endangered tree. Collection permits are available from the state's Bureau of Land Management as well as from the Forest Service. The Bureau of Land Management sells a Christmas-tree permit, for example, for $7.50; for that price, you can pick up branches for wreath-making along with a tree.

ABOVE: To make the Wyoming wreath, you'll need 3 circular double-wire wreath forms—8", 14", and 20"—and about 60 branches of pine. Start with the smallest form. Cut pine into branch tips 5" long. Wire these to the form using the wired-wreath technique described on page 19. For the 14" hoop, use bunches of branch tips 6" in length. The 20" form will take bundles of 8"-long tips. When you have finished wiring branches to wire forms, place the three hoops on top of one another so they fit together like a puzzle. Tie hoops together in four places using green floral wire: This will help them hang straight. To add pinecones, twist an eye hook into the bottom of each of seven cones. Thread floral wire through the eye hooks and attach to form. Trim excess wire.

Pinecones for Colorado's blue-spruce wreath (above) and Montana's
Ponderosa-pine wreath (opposite) are easily found on the forest floor. Use these rather than
taking cones from trees for wreath making. But first check local regulations.

LEFT: Start with an 18"-by-24" rectangular frame. Gather immature, hard oranges, grapefruit, lemons, limes, and kumquats (about 20 of each) and 5 bundles of lemon leaves. Secure floral wire on a paddle to a crossbar of the form. Lay a leaf bundle on the form, and wrap wire tightly around stems three times. Add another bundle by overlapping the previous one by half, and wrap wire around stems. Continue adding bundles until you reach the starting point. Tuck wire under form, secure, and cut. Prune the corners before adding the fruit.

BELOW: To attach the fruit, cut 20-gauge brass wire into 12" pieces; use 6" pieces for the kumquats. (Brass wire will give the wreath a jewel-like look.) Pierce the back half of each fruit with wire. Attach fruit to wreath form by threading wires through lemon leaves and frame. Twist wires and snip the ends.

FLORIDA (Citrus fruits) While Florida and orange juice seem inseparable, a natural duo like bacon and eggs, citrus fruits are not natives of the state. The Spanish explorer Ponce de Leon brought oranges with him on his voyage to Florida in 1513. As de Leon and his crew moved inland from St. Augustine, exploring the peninsula—and searching, according to legend, for a fountain of youth—they ate the Spanish oranges they'd brought with them, scattering seeds onto the sandy soil all the way down the coast. The subtropical climate, generous rainfall, and sunshine all made Florida a natural habitat for the fruit. Today, there are 900,000 acres of citrus groves in central and southern Florida, making the state the top producer of citrus in the country, with an $8 billion crop that also includes tangerines and grapefruit. Florida is so synonymous with citrus fruit that the baseball teams migrating to the state for spring training are known as the Grapefruit League, and from February to April, when the orange blossoms are in bloom, much of the state is permeated with the spicy fragrance of orange essence. What better materials for a wreath celebrating the home of the Orange Bowl?

FLORIDA
CITRUS FRUITS

ALASKA
SITKA SPRUCE

LEFT: The snowflake wreath can be made of sitka spruce or any other evergreen, such as Douglas fir. You will need a 32" snowflake form (see the Guide) and up to 600 branches. Each branch should be between 5" and 7" long. Make 100 bunches of 4 to 6 branches each. Sitka spruce can be prickly; wear work gloves when handling.

BELOW: Tie floral wire on a paddle to the tip of one branch of the snowflake form. Lay a neat bundle of sitka-spruce branches on a snowflake spoke (the bundle should extend 2" past the end of the spoke). Wrap floral wire around the bundle and the wreath spoke three times. Add another bundle to the spoke, overlapping the first bundle by half. Wrap the bundle three times with wire. Continue adding bundles in this fashion until you reach the center of the snowflake. Cut and secure wire. Go back and cover all off-shoots. Repeat this technique on the remaining snowflake spokes. Tuck more greenery into the wreath's center, and wire into place. Trim loose ends neatly with scissors.

ALASKA (Sitka spruce) You'd expect Alaska's state tree to be as strong and as indomitable as a Siberian husky, and you would be right. The sitka spruce *(Picea sitchensis)* is one of the world's most imposing trees, growing to a height of two hundred feet and living as long as six hundred years. The wood of the sitka spruce is so strong that Howard Hughes used it for his *Spruce Goose* aircraft; it is also used to make ship masts and musical instruments. Sitka spruce grows along the Alaskan coast on the islands and archipelagoes around the Icy Strait and Prince William Sound. It thrives in moisture and fog–temperate-rain-forest conditions, in other words. "I describe it as a cold-weather jungle," says Tim Bristol of the Southeast Alaska Conservation Council. "There's a really lush and dense understory below the canopy of big trees. It's just a different kind of rain forest." Unfortunately, much of the old-growth forests of sitka spruce are threatened by logging. There are federal restrictions against cutting live trees, so you can only gather branches from the forest floor or from trees that have fallen in storms.

TEXAS (Yellow roses) The wreath honoring this state combines two Texas icons: the Lone Star and the Yellow Rose of Texas. The wreath's shape was inspired by the white star on the Texas flag. Its color represents the Yellow Rose of Texas, who was not a flower but a woman and the central character in a story that is something of a Texas tall tale. Folklore has it that during the Texas battle for independence from Mexico, Emily Morgan, a slave to Texas revolutionary Col. James Morgan, was kidnapped by the Mexican general Antonio López de Santa Anna. Somehow, it's said, she secretly sent word to Sam Houston that Mexican forces were encamped at San Jacinto. In the legend, Santa Anna was dallying in his tent with the Yellow Rose when Houston's forces surprised and defeated him. In fact, though, the real Emily was Emily D. West, a free black woman from New York, who worked as a housekeeper for Morgan. There are no eyewitness accounts that link her to Santa Anna. Nevertheless, she inspired a classic song, "The Yellow Rose of Texas": "You may talk about your winsome maids and sing of Rosalie; But the Yellow Rose of Texas beats the belles of Tennessee."

ABOVE: The Texas wreath can be made from fresh or dried yellow roses (we used freeze-dried). You will need at least 60 flowers. To extend the stem of each rose, cut 24-gauge floral wire into 6" pieces. Place a wire at the top of a stem and wrap them together with green floral tape, going down the entire length of the stem.

RIGHT: The star-shaped wreath form is shaped by hand. The wreath we made needed 90" of 8-gauge floral wire. The wire was bent at 8½" increments into the star pattern shown. Pick any point on the star and place a yellow rose at a right angle to the frame, as shown in the photograph. Attach roses by wrapping the wire stem onto the frame, bending the wire so it's flush with the frame. Tightly wrap the wire to the frame with green floral tape. Do not cut the tape. Continue adding roses all around the star, keeping them at the same height. Bend the wire to follow around the corners of the star and cover with floral tape.

HAWAII (Orchids) "Love is worn like a wreath through the summers and the winters," goes a Hawaiian proverb. The lei, a necklace or wreath, is usually made with flowers, and has been a symbol of love, friendship, and what Hawaiians call the aloha spirit since the Polynesians first arrived here in the fifth century. Flowers pervade the Hawaiian culture. According to Kaniel Dan Akaka, a Hawaiian historian, the Hawaiian word for flower, *pua,* can also be used to describe the Hawaiian people–literally, "children of the islands." Leis can be made out of anything: flowers, seaweed, feathers, even dog's teeth. In ancient times, Hawaiian royalty wore leis of braided human hair. Far more amorous in spirit is the haku lei, used for celebrations and special occasions. Akaka describes it as a braided wreath made of plants and flowers gathered along the path to one's sweetheart's house; *haku* means to create and compose in the Hawaiian language. Since Hawaii's Big Island is the orchid-growing capital of the world, we created a giant lei, or wreath, of freshly cut orchids.

ABOVE: The Hawaii wreath was made with a variety of orchids— *Dendrobium, Cattleya, Cymbidium,* and *Vanda*—in assorted colors. You'll need about 100 orchid flowers to make this fragrant wreath. Each stem should be inserted into a plastic vial filled with water; orchids are usually sold this way. Stretch a 20" wire wreath form into an oval. Cover the wire frame by wrapping it with green floral tape as shown. Tape orchid stems at their midpoint onto the wreath form with green tape (do not tape the water vials). Position the water tubes behind the wreath form so they don't show. Refill the vials with water every two days to keep the flowers fresh. The wreath will last up to two weeks if the water is changed regularly.

U.S. TERRITORIES (Tropical leaves) The distinct cultures of Puerto Rico, the U.S. Virgin Islands, Guam, and American Samoa have one thing in common: a tropical climate. A wreath and a garland made of tropical leaves seemed an appropriate way to honor these territories as a group. In a way, these leaves are a testament to biological adaptation: In the hot climates in which they grow, the fact that they are both broad and thin allows them to capture what scarce light peeks through the dense forest canopy. The residents of these territories have adapted these leaves for myriad uses. In the Polynesian cultures of Guam and Samoa, ti leaves were once used to make capes and sandals. Other tropical leaves, such as banana, are used to wrap food for cooking. We used anthurium, banana, and ti leaves for our wreath and garland, but any large tropical leaves gathered locally, such as palm, will do.

ABOVE LEFT: You'll need 16 to 20 tropical leaves for the wreath. Start with a circular wreath form; ours was 36" wide. Attach floral wire diagonally across the form several times in a bicycle-spoke pattern. This is the base structure that will be covered with leaves. Fan the largest leaves around the wreath form as shown, leaving 2" stems facing the center. Tie each stem to the wire spokes on the form using 8" pieces of floral wire. Where a leaf meets the edge of the frame, secure its spine to the wreath form. Use a large needle and floral wire and sew the leaf spine to the form, making small stitches so they're not visible. Twist the ends of the wires together. To fill the center of the form, bunch about a dozen smaller leaves into a bouquet. Tie their stems together with floral wire, leaving the ends of the wire loose. Nestle the bouquet in the center of the wreath, and attach it by securing the wire to the form.

ABOVE RIGHT: To make the tropical-leaf garland, start with a piece of twine as long as you want the garland to be. You will need about 6 leaves (we used ti) for each foot of garland. Tie a paddle of floral wire to the twine. Wire two leaves onto the twine by wrapping them three times with floral wire. Continue adding two-leaf bunches without cutting the floral wire, overlapping each bunch by half as you move along the twine. Hang garland so the underside of the leaves face up.

ARKANSAS
RICE

ARKANSAS (Rice) In Arkansas, the country's major producer of rice (160 million bushels a year), the grain is an ingredient in just about anything: fruit salad, casseroles, even cheesecake. "Instead of potato salad you make a rice salad, and of course rice pudding is wonderful," says Helen Boyd, director of the Stuttgart Agricultural Museum in Arkansas County, where most of the state's rice fields are located. Since rice grows underwater, most of the state's paddies are in eastern Arkansas, which is flat and adjacent to riverbeds. A system of levees and gates guides fresh water, pumped from wells, into the fields. The water is drained when the rice matures. The levees follow the topography of the land, and from the air you can see their S-shaped curves running through the green fields of rice. The rice for our wreath was donated by Libbie Dougan, a grower in North Little Rock. "I cannot remember before rice, because we've always raised rice," says Dougan, who goes to church with Bill Clinton when the President is in Arkansas. "It's a good cash crop for us, and oh, my goodness, you can't know the green [of the rice] until you see it."

ABOVE: You'll need about 20 rice stalks for this wreath. They can be left in their natural state or painted gold with spray paint or a 3"-wide brush. If you paint them gold, as we did, you'll also need to paint the 8" single-wire wreath form gold to match. Attach 24-gauge brass wire on a paddle to the frame. Lay a rice stalk along the frame and wrap three times with brass wire. Add rice stalks halfway around the hoop as shown, each stalk overlapping the last one by a third. Return to starting point. With their tops facing the opposite direction, wire more stalks to the form until wreath is complete. The tips of each side should just barely meet. To hang the wreath, tie a ribbon where the stalk ends meet.

BELOW: Cut about 40 cotton bolls (pods) so that their stems are about 12" long. We made this wreath on a large scale with a 30" round wire wreath form. When the bolls are attached, it becomes even wider—about 45" diagonally—but the wreath can easily be scaled down using a smaller frame. Attach floral wire on a paddle to the form. Bunch about five cotton pods with stems and attach at the stems to the form by wrapping with floral wire three times. Without cutting the floral wire, continue adding bunches all around the wreath form. When finished, cut wire and secure.

ALABAMA (Cotton) Although the boll weevil did much to diminish Alabama's claim to be the Cotton State, the weevil is now nearly eradicated, and cotton, once again, is an important crop in the South. To be sure, the plant that fueled Alabama's economy for most of the nineteenth and much of the twentieth century never lost its hold on the culture and continues to be honored in song, in legend, and in memory. "There are more songs about cotton than any other crop," says Joe Dan Boyd, a folklorist and cotton editor for *Farm Journal,* reeling off titles like "Cotton Pickin' Hands," "Pick a Bale of Cotton," "Cotton Fields Back Home," and "Jesus Was Our Saviour (Cotton Was Our King)." And many people, especially those who grew up on or near farms, have fond memories of playing in the cotton as children. "We dug tunnels in the cotton, did flips in it," says Jamie Lazenby, Alabama representative for the National Cotton Women's Committee. "Stretching out on piles of picked cotton is warm and cozy, especially on a cool day." The variety known as American Upland cotton is what is grown on most farms in the state. The labor is no longer backbreaking since cotton picking is mostly mechanized, but King Cotton is still in the soul of the South.

Straw Forms

Padding a wire wreath form with straw or hay creates

a contoured base that can support a variety of materials. Leaves, dried flowers,

or even clamshells can then be pinned or glued onto the soft form,

creating a fuller, rounded shape. In fact, a wreath made of only straw or hay

is so beautiful that you may want to hang it on its own.

ABOVE LEFT: All of the wreaths in this chapter use a wire wreath form covered with straw. You'll need several armfuls of straw, which is readily available in bales at garden centers, riding stables, and some farmers' markets. Here is the basic technique for the wreaths in this chapter. STRAW-WREATH TECHNIQUE: Begin by attaching floral wire on a paddle to the crossbar of a metal wreath form. Pack a handful of straw against the form; hay can also be used. Wind wire tightly around the straw and the frame at 1" intervals all around the wreath. Repeat with additional handfuls until the form is completely covered.

ABOVE RIGHT: When the straw form is complete, cut floral wire with clippers and twist ends together at the back of the form. Use scissors or clippers to trim the straw for a smooth finish. To attach materials such as leaves or shells to a straw form, use floral pins, a hot-glue gun, or craft glue applied with a wooden Popsicle stick. To hang it from a nail, attach a length of wire to the back of the wreath. For heavier wreaths, use two nails.

CONNECTICUT (Mountain laurel)
Many Connecticut residents make a pilgrimage to the town of Union just to walk or drive through the Laurel Sanctuary at Nipmuck State Forest. This half-mile-long path cuts through a dense thicket of mountain laurel, Connecticut's state flower. "When it's in flower, it's spectacular," says Les Mehrhoff, the curator at the herbarium at the University of Connecticut at Storrs, "with very beautiful flowers that range from pure white to red." Mountain laurel *(Kalmia latifolia)* is an evergreen shrub that grows wild throughout the eastern United States and is also used as a common ornamental plant in gardens. No less beautiful than its June flowers are the mountain laurel's leaves, which are dark green and pointed at both ends. This simple wreath, decorated with four silver and gold mock bows, was inspired by neoclassical design, and is reminiscent of the laurel wreaths worn by victorious Olympic athletes in ancient Greece.

ABOVE: For the laurel wreath, pull 320 laurel leaves, uniform in size, off branches at their stems. The branches are available through florists. Mist the leaves. Prepare a straw-wreath form according to the instructions on page 50, using an 18" circular wreath form. With 1¼" floral pins, attach leaves near their stems to the straw form in a row. Attach the next row of leaves, overlapping half of the first row. Continue until form is completely covered with leaves. Mist wreath and wrap tightly with plastic for at least four hours or up to a day. This will flatten the leaves around the form. Remove the plastic before hanging. To extend the life of the wreath, spray-paint the dry leaves gold or silver.

RIGHT: To make the mock bows, you'll need 11' of 3"-wide gold ribbon and 8" of 1"-wide silver ribbon. Cut the gold ribbon into eight pieces, each 16" long. Cut the silver ribbon into four 2" pieces. Make a cross with two pieces of gold ribbon. Then place a 2" piece of silver ribbon where they intersect. Pinch the intersection, turn it over, and sew the silver ribbon tightly. Trim excess. Make three more. Evenly space the bows around the wreath, pinning ends of gold ribbon to underside of the form.

INDIANA (Peonies) There are few better weekends in Indiana than the Memorial Day holiday, and not just because that is when the Indianapolis 500 is held. On Memorial Day, almost all the peonies that grow all over Indiana burst into bloom. While they may look fragile, with their powder-puff blooms of coral, pink, and white, peonies are perennials, hardy enough to withstand Indiana winters of twenty degrees below zero. Leave a peony plant alone and it may live up to one hundred years with almost no upkeep. Peonies were cultivated in Asia more than two thousand years ago and arrived in the United States during colonial times, probably via England. The herbaceous peony *(Paeonia lactiflora)* became Indiana's state flower in 1957, and today more than 275 varieties grow there. In honor of these tough beauties, Indiana's wreath was made with freeze-dried peonies, which are available by mail order (see the Guide). Kept out of direct sunlight, the peony wreath will last for years.

ABOVE: To make the peony wreath, prepare a straw base as described on page 50, using a 30" metal wreath form. You will also need about 100 freeze-dried peonies of various colors, with stems attached. If a flower has no stem, create one: Insert an 8" wire through the base of the flower, bend the wire, and twist the ends together. Wrap floral tape from the base of the flower to the bottom of the wire. Use floral pins to attach flowers at their stems to the straw form, covering the stems as you go. Mix colors evenly around the wreath. Using floral pins allows you to change the position of the peonies on the wreath, but the flowers can also be attached to the straw form with a hot-glue gun.

SOUTH DAKOTA
HAY

ABOVE: Leftover shells from clam dishes (except broiled or baked dishes; the shells become brittle if put in the oven) can be used for this wreath. You'll need about 150 unbroken quahaug halves in both cherrystone (small) and littleneck (medium) sizes. Thoroughly clean out shells, then boil them for 30 minutes. If desired, soak overnight in a gallon of water with one cup of bleach to whiten. Wire straw to a 20" circular wreath form, using the technique on page 50. Work with five shells at a time, arranging them close together and overlapping them on the form. Place medium shells in the center and along the sides, tiny ones to fill in gaps. Hold shells in place temporarily by propping with straight pins. Pick up pinned shells one at a time; use a wooden Popsicle stick to spread extra-thick craft glue on the inside edge of shell. Replace on wreath. Keep pins in for support while wreath dries overnight, then remove. This wreath is heavy, so two nails should be used for hanging.

RHODE ISLAND (Quahaug shells)
Just about anyone who grew up in Rhode Island spent summers at the beach digging up buckets of hard-shell clams, or quahaugs (spelled q-u-a-h-o-g in the rest of the country). Almost 200,000 recreational clammers go looking for quahaugs every year on the tidal flats of Narragansett Bay. The word *quahaug* originated with Rhode Island's Narragansett Indians, who used the shells for wampum. The state's first colonial governor, Roger Williams, made special note of the quahaug in his register in 1643, describing the bivalve as a "little thick-shell fish which the Indians wade deep and dive for." This natural food resource went mostly untouched in the nineteenth century, when oystermen dominated the bay, but since the end of World War II, quahauging has been a big business. Today, nearly every Rhode Islander has a favorite recipe for stuffies, or baked stuffed quahaugs.

SOUTH DAKOTA (Hay) If the wind is blowing in the right direction on the Great Plains, the sweet smell of new-mown hay will waft for miles across this state. Today, this product of the grasslands is one of the largest agricultural industries of the state. Hay looks like straw but is actually a different product. Hay is mown grass; straw is the stem of grains such as wheat or barley after harvesting. In South Dakota, which is divided by the Missouri River, the hay that grows west of the river is native grass; east of the river, it is usually alfalfa. On either side, the hay grows green, waving in the wind up to eighteen inches high. When summer comes, the hay is cut, raked, and turned into square or round bales, which in turn are shipped across the nation for animal feed (and the occasional wreath).

ABOVE: The hay chandelier requires a bale of hay, a 5' wire wreath form, floral wire on a paddle or fishing line, a ball of strong twine or cord, 6 strands of 100 white or yellow holiday lights (with white cords), and an extension cord. Smaller forms can be used for smaller chandeliers. Use the straw-form technique described on page 50 to create the hay wreath; don't trim the hay. Connect the lights into one long rope and loosely wind them around the wreath, as you wound the floral wire. Plug the end into the extension cord. To make a triangular hanger for the chandelier, cut twine into three pieces about 3' long. Tie one end of each piece to the frame at three evenly spaced points. Knot pieces together; create a loop. Wind extension cord around one of the twine lengths. To hang, thread a long piece of twine through the loop and attach to two load-bearing beams. Continue winding extension cord around twine to the outlet. Don't leave lights on overnight.

WASHINGTON
MOSS

Living Wreaths

ARIZONA
CACTUS

Surely the most poetic of all wreaths is the living wreath.

More than an arrangement, it is a garden in miniature, one that changes constantly.

Many flowering plants, succulents, and grasses will adapt quite

well to this basic technique. Just water them regularly and watch them grow.

ABOVE: You can buy a living-wreath form ready to be planted (see the Guide) or you can fill one.
LIVING-WREATH TECHNIQUE: Tie a spool of 20-gauge copper wire to one end of a tubular
wreath form. Pack potting soil inside the core of the form, and continue until the entire
frame is filled. Surround the soil with sphagnum moss or other organic material and wrap with
copper wire. Add 2 small loops of copper wire to the back of the form for hanging the wreath.

LEFT: For the Washington moss wreath, prepare an 18" form according to the instructions on page 60. Pack small sections of moss around the sphagnum, then wrap with fishing line at 1" intervals to secure; tie off when finished. Hang wreath outside facing north. In dry weather, submerge wreath in water every two weeks for about two minutes. The wreath will last for months if kept moist.

BELOW: You'll need a variety of small cactus plants and cactus potting-soil mix to make the Arizona wreath. Stretch a 20" living-wreath form into an oval and fill, following directions on page 60. Use a pencil to poke holes into the moss and soil. Wearing heavy gloves to protect your hands, lift each cactus with tongs and place in hole. Use the pencil to push roots into soil. Support with floral pins without piercing cactus. Continue adding cactuses (clustering those with similar coloring, if desired) until entire wreath is covered. Wrap with fishing line at 1" intervals. Cut and tie off line. Leave wreath on a flat surface; water weekly until cactuses have rooted. After a month, the wreath should be ready to hang.

WASHINGTON (Moss) Although state boosters insist that Washington isn't as rainy as everybody thinks it is, western Washington is in fact one of the rainiest regions in the world, with some areas along the coast getting as much as 120 inches a year. While the rest of the state has a moderate and dry climate, the area west of the Olympic Mountains is the site of North America's only temperate rain forest. Botanists and geographers describe this area, where clouds hang low and the air is damp with mist, as the mossy forest, because it is ideal for the growth of woodland moss. Since mosses can't soak up water from soil, they must get their moisture from the air. There are hundreds of species of mosses native to Washington, from the terrestrial kind that grow in mats at the base of trees to others that hang in festoons from tree limbs. We used a variety of terrestrial mosses to make the wreath in honor of Washington. Moss is often protected, but it is available at florists or by mail order (see the Guide).

ARIZONA (Cactus) Cactuses have been growing in the southwestern United States for millions of years, and the cactus is such an icon here that one of the state's novelty license plates is emblazoned with an image of the saguaro, one of the biggest cactuses of all. In fact, there are more cactuses growing in Arizona than in any other state, and the blossom of the saguaro is the state flower. "You don't walk out in the desert here without looking down," says Linda Wallace Gray, who is with the Nature Conservancy in Tucson. "When you hike, you carry a comb and a pair of pliers to pull the spines out of your legs. Most of us think of cactus as beautiful, anyway." The spines of the cactus, as well as its thick flesh and odd shapes, are the plant's evolutionary adaptation to strong sunlight, heat, and drought. We created a living wreath of small varieties of cactus such as the *Opuntia, Echinocereus,* and *Mammillaria,* which can be bought from garden centers. You can also find cactus plants in supermarkets.

WISCONSIN (Violet) Wood violets grow wild in Wisconsin, from the woods and bogs of the southern Baraboo Hills to just about every lawn. In fact, this state's official flower often turns up out of nowhere. The reason, says Harvey Ballard, a botanist at the University of Wisconsin at Madison, is that violets have an uncanny ability to reproduce, in part because ants carry their seeds from one spot and drop them in another. Ballard says he has observed a new mutation of the Wisconsin wood violet spreading from yard to yard straight down his block. This mutation is called "Freckles," because its pale lavender flowers are speckled with tiny purple spots. Any of Wisconsin's twenty native species of wood violet is appropriate for its state wreath. Just dig up whole clumps from your backyard (or buy violets at a garden center), assemble the wreath, and keep it watered.

KENTUCKY (Bluegrass) "Blue moon of Kentucky keep on shining," wrote Bill Monroe, who in the forties named his band—Bill Monroe and His Blue Grass Boys—after the grass that grows in meadows across central Kentucky. Monroe's music sparked an entire genre called bluegrass, with its heartfelt country tunes, its banjos, and its fiddles. As residents of the state like to point out, their famous grass is not blue but dark green, except in May, when the dwarf iris and wild columbine are in bloom, giving the grass a bluish cast. As synonymous as it is with the state, bluegrass did not originate in Kentucky; it came to America in the seventeenth century mixed with soil brought over on European ships. Kentucky was the first place where bluegrass seed was grown for commercial production as a turf grass. It is now so beloved that the official nickname of Kentucky is "The Bluegrass State."

ABOVE: The wood-violet wreath can be made on a double-ring form, as shown, or on a tubular living-wreath form. For the former, wrap wet leaves or other organic matter around the roots of a clump of violets. Some dirt should be clinging to the roots. Secure the violets by wrapping with copper wire at 1" intervals around the form. Repeat, bunching plants close together. Cut wire and tie off. Leave the wreath outside on a flat surface for about a week to let plants take root. Keep soil damp.

If you're using a living-wreath form, which is particularly good for young plants (they can grow to maturity on the form), follow the instructions for preparing a living wreath on page 60. Poke holes in the soil using a pencil, and insert the roots of the violets. Wrap wire around the form at 1" intervals to secure. Leave the wreath outside on a flat surface for a week, keeping soil damp. Once the roots have taken, hang the wreath and water it regularly. Outdoors, the wreath should live through the season.

ABOVE: Bluegrass has a dense root system and therefore takes well to a living wreath. The Kentucky wreath can be made with either sod or seeds. To make the wreath with sod, shown here, first grow bluegrass in a flat. Bluegrass is slow-growing; allow several weeks for it to reach a height of 4 to 6 inches. When grass is ready, fill an 18" living-wreath form with potting soil. Attach copper wire to the frame, cut bluegrass into small clumps of sod, and place on form. Secure by wrapping copper wire around form at 1" intervals. Cut wire and tie to form.

To make the wreath with seeds, tie a spool of 20-gauge copper wire to one end of an 18" living-wreath form. Fill with potting soil, and scatter seeds evenly onto the soil. Surround with sphagnum moss and wrap with the copper wire at 1" intervals. Cut wire and tie to form. Keep the wreath wet until grass begins to grow, then water regularly.

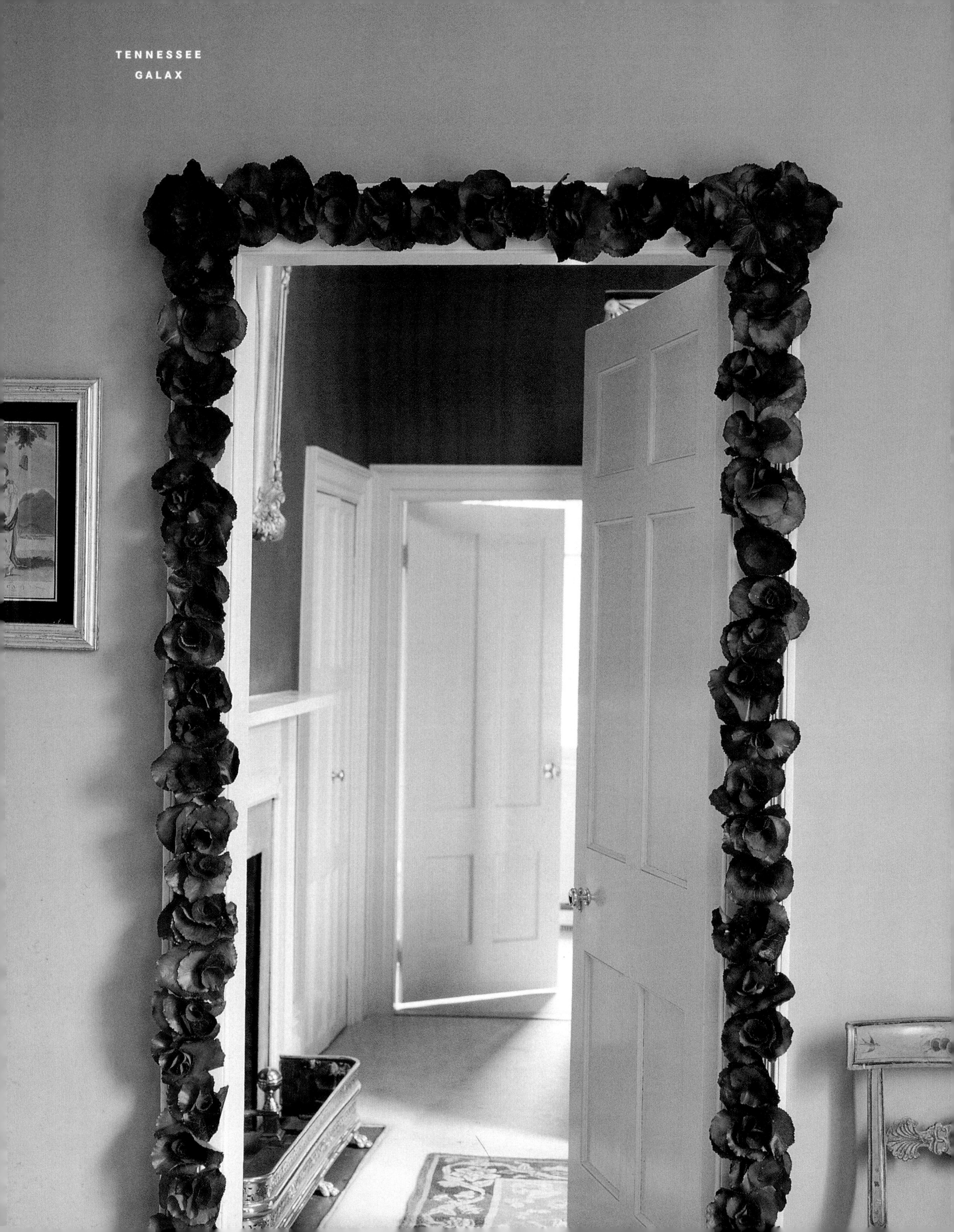

Swags and Garlands

LOUISIANA
MAGNOLIA

Garlands and swags have been used since ancient times, when the

Greeks decorated their houses and temples with bands of leaves and flowers.

Flowers and foliage become a garland when woven into a chain;

drape the garland between two points gracefully and you have a swag.

LOUISIANA (Magnolia) In Louisiana, the evergreens called *Magnolia grandiflora* are so abundant that the Cajuns substitute magnolia leaves for palms on Palm Sunday. These graceful trees grow all over the state—from ridge tops to the Mississippi River Road—thanks to birds and squirrels that spread their seeds. "They won't grow in water, but they'll grow just about anywhere else," says Ken Durio of the Louisiana Nursery in Opelousas, which cultivates dozens of varieties of southern magnolia. The magnolia is Louisiana's state flower, but its leaves are equally noteworthy: dark green in color, as smooth as leather, and from five to eighteen inches in length. We wove magnolia leaves into one long garland, draped it over an entrance, and accented it with a rosette of seedpods.

TENNESSEE (Galax) Most Americans have seen galax, even if they haven't heard of it. This native ground cover, which grows in Tennessee's Appalachian Mountains, is used by florists all over the country to camouflage the bases of centerpieces. Few plants have lovelier leaves than *Galax urceolata (aphylla),* which are fan-shaped with ruffled edges. In summer, they are glossy and green; in fall, they turn a beautiful rusty bronze, like the leaves used in the garland we made for Tennessee, and remain that way throughout the winter. Galax has been popular as holiday greenery since the turn of the century, when it was a principal source of income for the women who lived in the Appalachian Mountains. As the winter holidays approached, the women would gather the galax, still green under the ice and snow, and give it to their husbands to take to town to sell as decorations.

ABOVE: Begin the Louisiana garland by cutting a piece of twine to desired length; this garland is 20' long. Tie floral wire on a paddle to one end of twine. Arrange bunches of leafy branches 4" thick around twine; secure by wrapping with floral wire. Continue until twine is covered. Place 7 magnolia leaves with their stems attached on garland base; wrap with floral wire three times to secure. Repeat, covering stems, until base is completely covered— about 100 bunches of magnolia leaves for this garland. To make center rosette (see page 67), cluster additional magnolia leaves around 6 seedpods and wire tightly into a bouquet. Hang the garland from 2 nails on a doorway and attach rosette at midpoint.

OPPOSITE: For the Tennessee garland, we used 600 galax leaves with stems attached, obtained from a florist shop. Twist a small leaf into a tight cone and secure by wrapping it tightly with brown floral tape from the base to about 2" down the stem. Wrap a second leaf around the cone and tape. Continue adding leaves, about 8 in all, to make a rosette. Cut floral wire to a length of 18", fold in half, and wind it halfway down the stem clusters. Cut twine to desired length of garland (ours was 19' long and used about 75 rosettes; smaller versions can be made). Attach 24-gauge floral wire on a paddle to twine. Lay a rosette on the twine and wrap wire around stems and twine three times. Continue wiring on successive rosettes, about 3" apart, until twine is covered. When finished, arrange rosettes by bending wire away from twine.

LOUISIANA
MAGNOLIA

NORTH DAKOTA (Oats and barley)
North Dakota, which leads the nation in oat and barley production, often celebrates its grain harvest with threshing bees. At these community festivals, North Dakotans learn to gather and thresh grain the old-fashioned way, by scooping up bundles of grain by the armful and throwing them into antiquated steam tractors, says Lance Gaebe, executive director of the North Dakota Grain Growers Association. Oats are grown throughout the state, and at harvesttime, the North Dakota countryside smells distinctly of oatmeal. Half of the barley produced in North Dakota is used for animal feed, but in the northern part of the state, barley is grown for malting and used to make beer or distilled liquors such as whiskey. Inspired by North Dakota's yearly threshing bees, we created two huge swags of oats and barley that could be hung over the entrance to a barn.

ABOVE LEFT: We made the North Dakota garlands and fan decoration on a massive scale to fit a particular doorway, but they can easily be reduced in size. We added 2' to each garland so they would drape onto the floor. You will need 2700 oat stalks and a spool of twine for our version. Separate the oats into 90 bunches of 30 stalks. Cut each bundle 3" below the base of the oat head. Unravel twine to desired length. Attach floral wire on a paddle by winding around the end of the twine. Secure the first bundle to twine with floral wire. Knot the wire but do not cut.

ABOVE CENTER: Cluster the next oat bunch around the twine, completely covering twine, and wrap floral wire around the stems three times to secure. Continue wiring oat bundles along the twine, staggering the bunches so each new one covers the stalk of the previous bunch, as shown. Cut wire and secure.

ABOVE RIGHT: To make the fan decoration, you will need about 50 stalks of barley. The stems should be trimmed to a length of 3". Cut a semicircle out of corrugated cardboard; its diameter should be half the width of the door's transom (ours was 15" in diameter). Glue barley to cardboard as shown, overhanging edge of cardboard by about ½". Cover the bottom of the stems by gluing on oat stalks with their stems cut off.

OPPOSITE: Tack the fan above the doorframe. Place two nails over the door where the garland ends meet and a nail on each side of frame. Hang the garlands over the nails so they drape evenly onto the floor. The garlands will last a long time if properly stored: Place them in a cardboard box lined with tissue paper and mothballs, then store in a larger box and keep in a dry place.

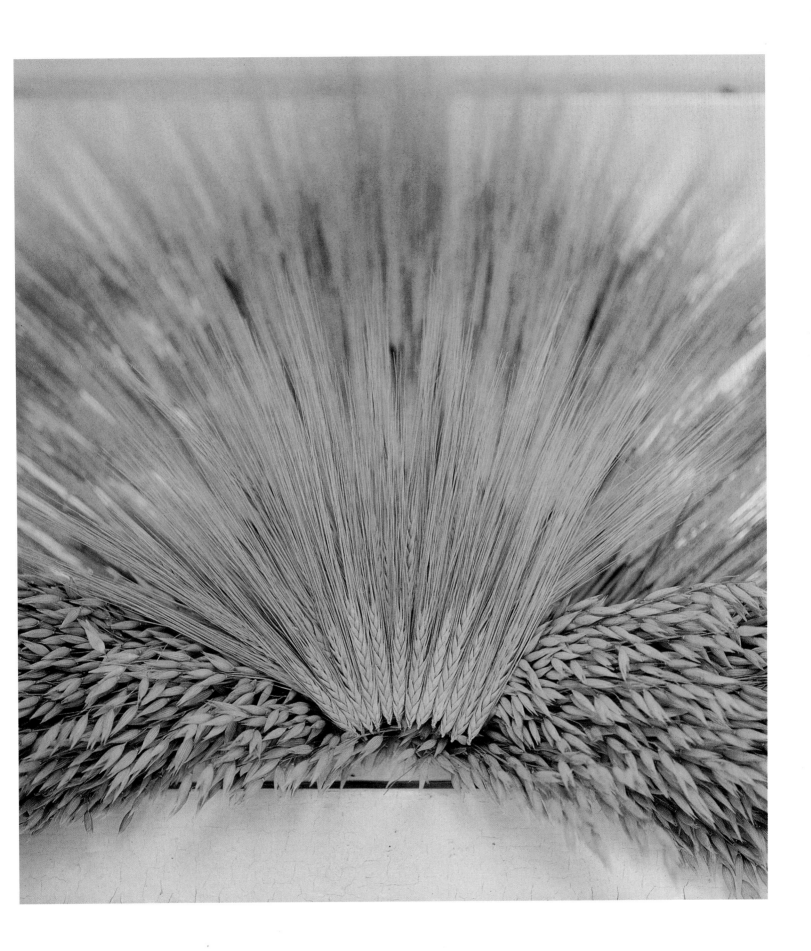

NEBRASKA (Miniature Indian corn) For Nebraska's Native Americans, each color of corn is symbolic. The Ponca tribe, for example, believes that yellow symbolizes the start of life, and blue the end of life. Red represents strength. Judi Morgan, executive director of Nebraska's Indian Commission, who is half Ponca and half Santee-Sioux, says corn was a staple for the elders in her tribe, who subsisted all winter on *wah-sna,* a Ponca recipe in which dried corn is mixed with dried buffalo or beef and dried chokecherries. "They hung the mix in flour bags and ate it during the months when food was sparse," she says. Nebraska's pioneers started growing corn in the late nineteenth century. Thanks to advances in irrigation technology in the 1950s, Nebraska now grows more than a billion bushels of corn a year on its prairie. Our swag of miniature Indian corn honors the role of this crop in Nebraska's Native American history as well as its importance as an agricultural commodity.

ABOVE: This swag of miniature Indian corn can be made to any length: Our swag of 64 ears of corn was made to run the length of a large window. Select an assortment of 3"-long ears of corn in several colors, with husks attached. We placed the corn in a repeating color pattern as we made the swag. To start, take three 2' strands of raffia, place one ear of corn in the middle, and tightly tie a knot around husks. Make 3 or 4 loose knots before adding next ear to create "links" in the swag. Continue adding corn and knots until about 3" of raffia remains. Take 3 new strands of raffia and center them on top of the last knot made, so that tails of the new raffia strands overlap the old strands. Twist old and new strands together. Depending on where you are in the swag, either knot in the next ear of corn or continue creating links. Add corn until you reach desired length. Trim raffia ends when you're done.

MISSOURI
BLACK WALNUTS

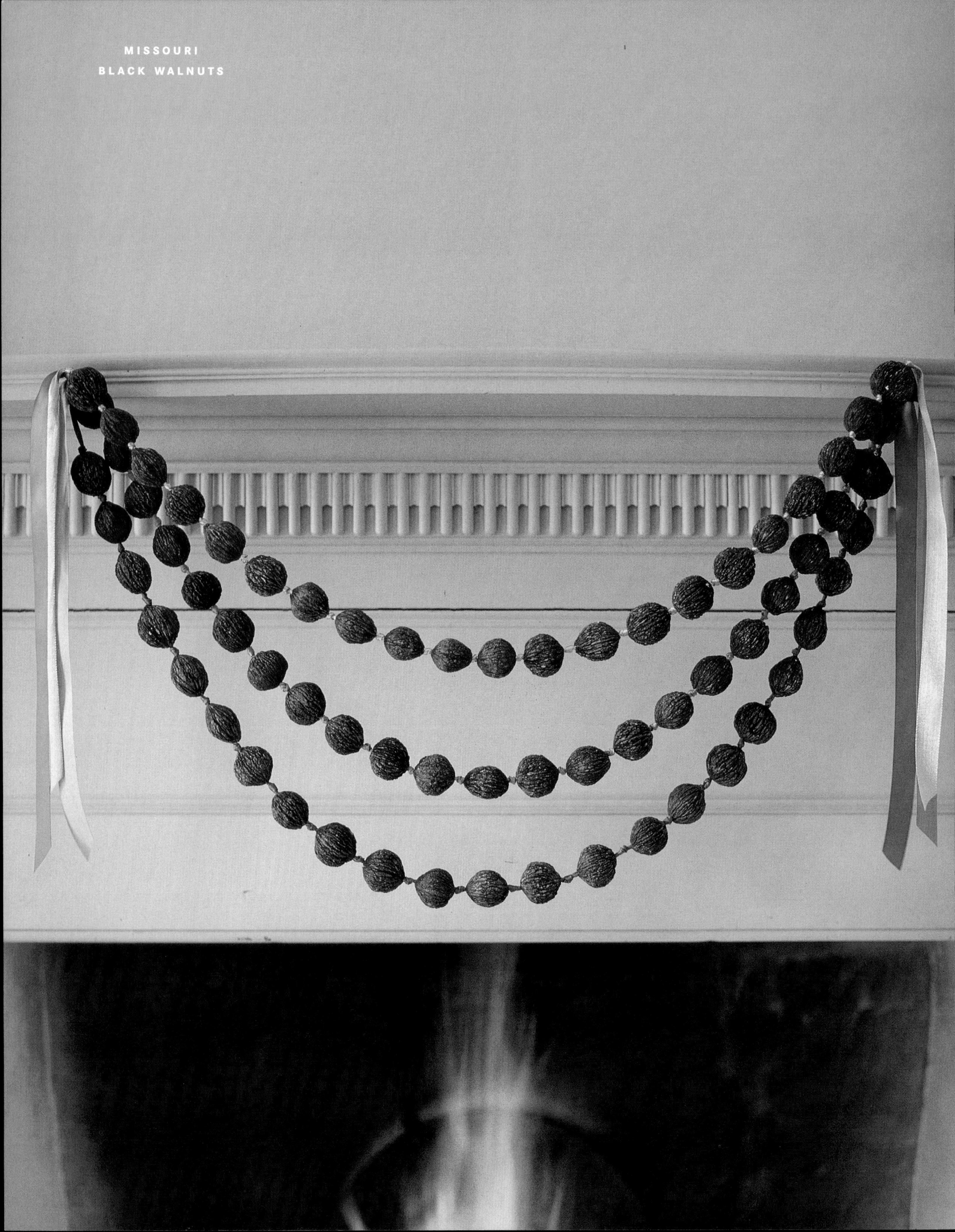

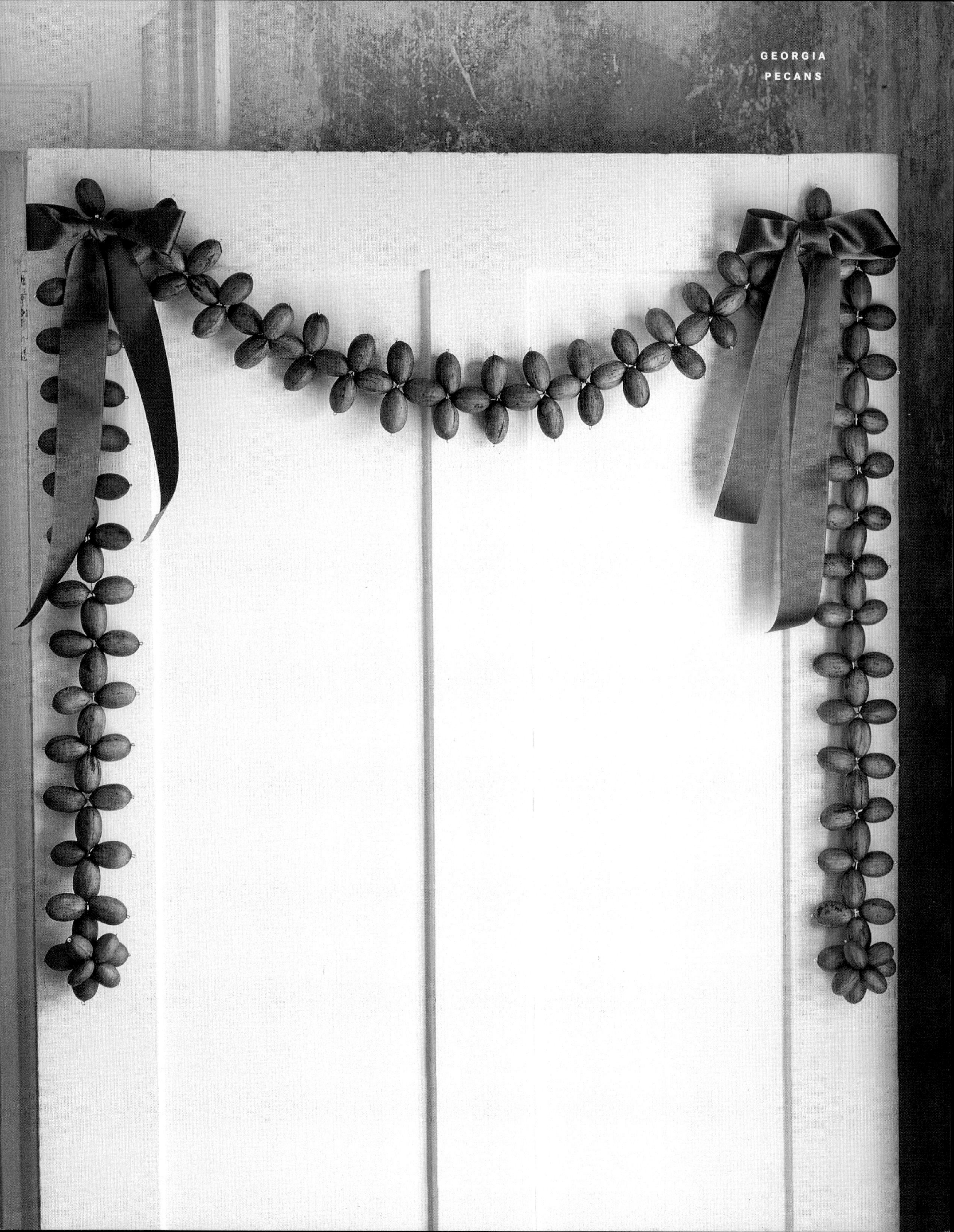

OPPOSITE, TOP LEFT: For the Georgia swag, you will need about 200 large pecans, uniform in size, and a drill with a ⁵⁄₆₄" bit. Measure the width of the door, then add 4'6". Cut 20-gauge brass wire to this length. With a rag, coat pecans with tung oil (a hardware-store staple) to give them a sheen; let dry and repeat.

OPPOSITE, TOP RIGHT: Drill a hole lengthwise through each nut.

OPPOSITE, BOTTOM LEFT: String pecans onto wire, alternating point to point and rounded end to rounded end. Place pairs of pecans, points facing together, on 5" wire sections. Put a short-wire section at a right angle between each pecan on long wire, wrapping once around to create a flower effect. Push the pairs of pecans together. Snip wire ends, leaving ¼" on each side.

OPPOSITE, BOTTOM RIGHT: Twist ends into loops with round-nose pliers. To finish garland ends, choose eight small pecans. Put 2 on each wire. Take 2 of these wires and twist them into a rosette shape. Attach with floral wire to ends of garland. Drape the swag on a door or frame, and nail into place.

BELOW: Missouri's swag of black walnuts has three strands of different color ribbon and uses 70 nuts in all. The top (gold) was 33" long, the middle (teal) was 38", and the bottom (royal blue) was 40". Start by cutting ribbon to twice the desired length of the swag. Knot the ribbon, leaving a tail of 15". Use a drill with a ⅛" bit to make a hole through each walnut. Fold an 8" piece of brass floral wire in half. Use this to push the long end of the ribbon through the hole of a black walnut as shown. Tie another knot as close to the walnut as possible and continue adding nuts until desired length of swag is reached. Repeat for the two other swags, then hang like a three-strand necklace, as pictured on page 76. Cut the tails of the ribbons so they are equal on both sides.

GEORGIA (Pecans) Five hundred varieties of pecan grow in the United States, mostly in the state of Georgia. The pecan (*Carya illinoiensis*), a member of the hickory family, originally grew wild in the Mississippi Valley region of the country. Pecans are thought to have been introduced to Georgia by Native Americans, who have used the nut since pre-Columbian times; pecan is an American Indian word that appears in the languages of several tribes. Both George Washington and Thomas Jefferson planted pecan trees on their estates. The first large commercial pecan groves were in Georgia; as a tribute to this state's $80-million industry, the runners who carried the Olympic flame to Atlanta in the summer of 1996 carried torch handles made from Georgia pecan trees.

MISSOURI (Black walnuts) When autumn's first cold snap hits west-central Missouri, it signals everyone that black walnuts are ready to be harvested. The Black Walnut Festival, held in Stockton each year in late September, honors this important crop, whose meat and shells are both useful. The black walnut (*Juglans nigra*) is native to North America and gets its name from the dark husk that grows around the nut. The nutmeat is pale in color, not black, and has a strong, slightly sweet taste that is good in ice cream, cakes, and cookies. Compared to Persian walnuts, their thinner-shelled European cousins, black walnuts are notoriously difficult to shell (for the determined, a hammer and a nutpick does the job). In fact, the shells are used in industry as an abrasive to clean ship exteriors and jet engines. On a much gentler level, cosmetic companies often add pulverized black-walnut shells to facial scrubs.

Missouri's black-walnut swag (above) is knotted like a pearl necklace: Each nut is separated by a
knot as it is strung along the ribbon. This swag of Georgia pecans (opposite) is finished off at the ends with rosettes,
each consisting of eight pecans—smaller than those used for the swag—that are wired together.

Twig Wreaths

A twig wreath is as close as your own backyard. Clip some branches

from a favorite tree, twist them into a circle, and you have the most natural wreath of all.

A twig wreath makes a fine base for many materials; of course,

some purists like its rudimentary charm so much that they hang it unadorned.

ABOVE LEFT: The wreaths in this chapter are all based on a version of this frame. You can use grapevine or any deciduous tree branches—each branch has to be freshly cut in order to be flexible enough to bend.

TWIG-WREATH TECHNIQUE: Strip a long branch of its leaves and bend it into a circle. Twist the ends together so they stay secure. Add three more long branches, intertwining them into the first circle and weaving the ends together. When ever working with a twig base, it's a good idea to wear gloves to protect your hands.

ABOVE RIGHT: New York's rose-hip wreath begins with a twig or vine base as described in the technique above. Attach floral wire on a paddle to the base. Clip off fully fruited rose-hip branch tips (we used *Rosa multiflora*), leaving 5" of stem. (Rose-hip branches are readily available at florists and garden centers.) You will need about 60 tips. Bunch 4 or 5 tips and lay them on the form. Attach by wrapping three times with wire. Do not cut wire. Continue wiring bundles around the form until the form is completely covered. Cut wire and secure. Thread a 2"-wide red ribbon through the back of the twig wreath and hang.

LEFT: Begin the dogwood wreath by making a twig base with freshly cut deciduous branches, as described on the opposite page. Cut about 75 dogwood branch tips and strip the leaves; cut into 6" lengths. (Dogwood trees are relatively small, so feel free to use other types of branches.) Tie floral wire on a paddle to the twig form. Lay a bundle of 6 or 8 branch tips on the form. Wrap floral wire around the stems and wreath form three times. Do not cut the wire. Continue adding bundles of tips, overlapping the previous ones by half, all the way around. Cut wire and secure.

BELOW: Use a hot-glue gun to attach about 60 dried white dogwood blooms to the branches. The blooms are available by mail order (see the Guide) or you can dry your own by pressing them between heavy books for three weeks. Humidity will cause the blooms to wilt, so make and hang the wreath in a dry environment.

NEW YORK (Rose hips) In New York, where the rose is the official state flower, rose hips appear on wild rose bushes after the flowers have fallen off. Rose hips have been called the "apple of the rose" because like apples, they are the fruit of the bush, ripening through the summer until they turn a deep scarlet. Different rose bushes produce different hips, from the peppercorn-size hips of *Rosa multiflora* to the cherry-size fruit of *R. rugosa.* Most are packed with vitamin C, and as Euell Gibbons wrote in *Stalking the Healthful Herbs,* quite tasty in jam or soup. For New York's wreath, we used rose hips from *R. multiflora,* a Japanese plant introduced in the United States in the 1930s to hedge fields. In the decades since, *R. multiflora* has grown so vigorously throughout New York state that it is not appreciated by everybody. Many farmers consider it a weed. "It's really quite pretty and great for wildlife," says Bruce Lund, a naturalist with the Nature Conservancy on Long Island. "The problem is that it is very aggressive and will take over a pasture that's not grazed or mowed." While no one would recommend planting any new *R. multiflora,* there is plenty available all over New York, and the crimson-colored hips do look lovely in a wreath.

VIRGINIA (Dogwood) George Washington loved the flowering dogwood tree (*Cornus florida),* as did Thomas Jefferson, who planted dogwoods on the lawn at Monticello. In fact, few Virginians are unmoved by the sight of the dogwood when its white and pink flowers appear, announcing the arrival of spring. These blooms are not petals but bracts surrounding the dogwood's less noticeable true flowers. The bracts form the shape of a cross, and in the South, legend has it that they symbolize the Crucifixion. The wood from the tree is extraordinarily hard and has been used for making golf-club heads, chisel handles, and weaving shuttles. According to Chris Ludwig, staff botanist for the Virginia Department of Conservation's Division of Natural Resources, dogwood is not an endangered species, so it can be gathered on public lands. Since dogwood is the state flower, however, many Virginians feel strongly about protecting it. And in recent years, this native tree has been threatened by dogwood anthracnose, a rampant fungal disease. But instead of disappearing the way the American chestnut did, the dogwood is enduring. In celebration of this survivor and native treasure, we made a wreath out of the dogwood's branches and its white blooms.

CALIFORNIA
OLIVE AND ROSEMARY BRANCHES,
GRAPEVINES

LEFT: To make the New Mexico wreath, create a twig circle 6" in diameter with any available freshly cut branches, following the directions on page 84. Attach raffia or twine to the twig frame. Create a small bundle of fresh sagebrush, leaving stems about 4" long. Wrap raffia cord three times around the bundle as shown. Continue adding sagebrush, overlapping previous bundle by half, until frame is covered. Cut raffia and secure by knotting. To finish the wreath, pin a bow of sage-green velvet ribbon to the top.

BELOW AND OPPOSITE: The base of the California wreath is made from two bundles of eight 5'-long grapevine branches, but a wreath of smaller proportions could be made. Cross the branches just above their bases and secure with floral wire. Gather 10 branches each of flowering rosemary and fully fruited olive branches. The branches should be 16" to 24" long. Attach floral wire on a paddle to the top of one side of the frame. Wire one branch of rosemary to the grapevine, wrapping wire around it three times. Continue adding rosemary branches, overlapping previous one by half. Stop at the intersection. Use this wiring technique to attach olive branches to the other half.

NEW MEXICO (Sagebrush)

The desert plant *Artemisia ludoviciana,* also called western sage, has been prized for its aromatic, silvery foliage in the New Mexico region for more than two thousand years. Navajo and Pueblo Indians have long used it for "smudging" ceremonies in which they burn its leaves, take the smoke in their hands, and rub the smoke over their bodies. This ritual is thought to drive out bad spirits or feelings. The camphor in sagebrush makes it highly valued in treating colds and coughs; it is often boiled in water and the steam inhaled as a decongestant. About thirty varieties of artemisia grow wild in New Mexico, where the plant is so admired that many people use it to landscape their gardens. We made New Mexico's wreath out of *A. tridentada,* or sagebrush, which grows to heights of more than ten feet, and is common in the northern Rio Grande valley near Taos.

CALIFORNIA (Olive and rosemary branches, grapevine) This state's cuisine, with its emphasis on local ingredients, inspired a wreath of olive and rosemary branches attached to an armature of grapevines. The grapevines represent the state's wine industry, which is concentrated in the Napa and Sonoma Valleys of Northern California. The olive branches are a symbol of the state's groves of olive trees, the oldest of which were introduced to California centuries ago by Franciscan missionaries from Spain. As for the rosemary, Alice Waters, the chef-owner of Chez Panisse restaurant, in Berkeley, says that this perennial herb grows practically wild in California. There are creeping, trailing varieties and more upright, bushy varieties. Waters likes to add fresh rosemary to onions and potatoes, and she uses the sturdy straight branches of the upright variety as skewers for grilled meat, fish, or poultry.

MINNESOTA
RED NORWAY PINE

LEFT: Make the Minnesota wreath by wiring together five 2'-long freshly cut sticks from any tree, in the star shape as shown. Tie a length of rope to the center of the star for hanging, wrap it around the entire length of one of the sticks, and secure rope to end of stick with floral wire.

BELOW: You'll need about 40 bundles of ten 6" pine branches for the star. Tie floral wire on a paddle to the end of a stick. Lay a neat bundle of pine branches on the stick. Wrap floral wire and a string of white lights around the stems three times. Place another bundle on the stick, overlapping the first by half, and wrap with wire and lights. Continue adding bundles and wrapping lights until the entire frame is covered. (You can also wrap the lights around the star after the greenery has been added.) Run an extension cord around the rope; hang wreath and plug in lights.

MINNESOTA (Red Norway pine)
The motto of Minnesota, "L'Etoile du Nord," meaning the North Star, was chosen by the state's first governor, Henry Sibley–a reminder that many French explorers, missionaries, and fur traders helped settle the state in the mid-seventeenth century. Acquired from France as a part of the Louisiana Purchase, Minnesota became a state in 1858. Our wreath for Minnesota is in the shape of a three-dimensional star. Its frame is covered with branches of Minnesota's state tree, red Norway pine (*Pinus resinosa*), which gets its common name from the reddish-brown hue of its bark. The needles of the red pine are long and slender. Minnesota basket weavers use a coiling technique to make red-pine-needle baskets. Native American children use the needles to make dolls, which they place upright on a sheet of birch bark. By gently moving the bark, the red-pine dolls appear to dance like adults at a powwow.

Pointing the way home: hang the Minnesota North Star wreath from the front porch, and cover the railing with additional pine branches and lights.

WEST VIRGINIA (Rhododendron)
West Virginia was settled later than
the states that surround it, in 1863,
and rhododendron is in some measure
responsible. In the early days of the
colonies, these evergreen trees and
shrubs, with their gnarled branches and
crooked trunks, formed an impassable
thicket through much of West Virginia.
"It was so thick and dense that men
would get lost in it and horses couldn't
get through it," says Paul J. Harmon,
botanist for the West Virginia Natural
Heritage Program. "The Indians wouldn't
even go through it. It was called 'the
hells.'" Logging at the turn of the century
diminished some of the rhododendron,
but there are still plenty of the shrubs,
which are called Big Laurel by people in
the mountains. "One of my colleagues
says you couldn't get rid of it if you beat
it with a stick," says Harmon. The pale-
pink flowers of the *Rhododendron
maximum* are the state flower, and West
Virginia's flag is decorated with a
wreath of rhododendron leaves. Taking
the state flag as our inspiration, we
made the West Virginia wreath with the
oblong leaves of the *R. maximum*.

ABOVE: To make the West Virginia wreath base, you'll need 4
rhododendron branches trimmed of foliage, two 21" long and two
8" long (other tree branches can be used). Cross the two longer
branches and secure at center with twine. Use the two shorter
branches for crossbars and attach with twine, creating a bow-tie-
shaped frame as shown. Attach floral wire on a paddle to the form.

OPPOSITE: Gather twenty-four 3'-long branches of rhododendron
with leaves attached. Strip the branches, leaving only the foliage
at the top. Starting at one end of the frame, secure the branches
to the form by wrapping with floral wire. Use some of the
branches to create new supports, as shown in the photograph, on
which you continue wiring branches. Keep going until one side
of the frame is covered with leaves, then repeat on the other side.
Cover the intersection of the bow tie by wrapping it with a wide
ribbon. Hang the wreath on 2 nails or use transparent fishing line
to suspend it from an existing nail.

UTAH
MIXED EVERGREENS

LEFT: To make the Utah wreath base, cut two 4' branches from any tree (the branches should be 1" to 2" thick and stripped of foliage). Drill a small hole through the centers, cross branches, and screw together. Drill holes at each end of four 9"-long, ½"-thick sticks, form into a square, and screw to crossbars at corners, as shown at left. Cross two 15" twigs, lay over square, and drill holes where twigs cross square; attach with screws.

BELOW: Gather 10 bundles each of Rocky Mountain juniper with berries and limber, lodgepole, and ponderosa pines (or four other evergreens of your choice), with pinecones attached, if possible. If the branches don't have pinecones attached, obtain 15 to 20 loose ones. Each bundle should have six 6"-long branches. Using floral wire on a paddle, attach the juniper to the center square and smaller crossbars. Attach the mixed pines to the longest crossbars as desired; we created a deliberate pattern to show off the different colors and textures of the pines. Wire in pinecones at various intervals, and wire several pinecones into the juniper in the center of the wreath (see picture, opposite).

UTAH (Mixed evergreens) Few states vary in topography as much as Utah, with its ski resorts in the north and desert mesas of the Canyonlands to the south. We made Utah's wreath out of four evergreens that grow across the state. Skyrocket, a variety of *Juniperus scopulorum,* is a tall column-shaped tree that looks like a blue rocket from a distance and grows in the Canyonlands. Limber pine grows in the higher, cooler elevations of the Rocky Mountains. Its scientific name is *Pinus flexilis* because its branches are so flexible they can be tied in knots. *P. ponderosa,* a classic conifer of the American West, grows in the drier part of the state. Lodgepole pine, *P. contorta latifolia,* grows in the Rocky Mountains at altitudes of eight to ten thousand feet, and gets its common name from the fact that Native Americans use its wood for their tepee poles.

DELAWARE
AMERICAN HOLLY

WASHINGTON, D.C. (White oak)
The oak has always connoted power
and solidity. In ancient Rome, wreaths
of oak leaves symbolized the rank of
rulers, and today it is no less appropriate
that so many oaks grow in Washington,
D.C., appearing everywhere from the
White House lawn to the Lincoln Memorial. In honor of the nation's capital, we
designed a classically inspired wreath
and made it out of the leaves and acorns
of the white oak (*Quercus alba*). Various
species of oak are indigenous to most
of the United States. Of all of them,
however, white oak is the most majestic,
says Matthew Evans, the Landscape
Architect of the Capitol. "I love it for its
almost dark-blue leaves and its very
airy, open, and wide branching habit,"
he says. "Anyone who visits the Capitol
grounds will be in for a treat to see
some of our mature white oaks."

ABOVE LEFT: Collect 10 oak leaves and 10 acorns, both with
stems attached. You'll also need several sheets of 24-karat gold
leaf and sizing glue, both available at art-supply stores. Let acorns
dry until they turn brown. Remove caps, then reattach with
wood glue so they don't fall off once the wreath is assembled. To
gild acorns, coat first with sizing glue, using a small soft paintbrush. Allow to dry for two hours. Cut off a small piece of gold
leaf, and cover acorn with gold leaf using tweezers. To impress it
on to the surface, rub it, using the back of the paintbrush, your
fingernail, or any other small burnishing tool.

ABOVE CENTER: Press the leaves overnight between two heavy
books to flatten. To add luster and a bit of color to the leaves,
paint both sides with a dark wood stain such as Minwax "Ja-
cobean." Let dry overnight. (For more a golden effect, you can
spray paint the leaves with gold paint, as shown on page 14.)

ABOVE RIGHT: Place a 12" piece of floral wire alongside an oak-
leaf stem. Tightly wrap together the stem and wire with brown
floral tape to cover the length of the wire. Repeat for remaining
leaves. Glue a 6" piece of floral wire to the stub of an acorn cap.
Let dry, then cover the wire with floral tape. Repeat for remaining acorns. Lay out the leaves and acorns in two sections, as
shown on page 98. Starting with the leaf that will be at the top
of the wreath, wrap the wired stems together, alternating leaves
and acorns. This will create a "branch." Be sure to leave 1" or 2"
of stem between each leaf and acorn and the branch. When finished with both branches, cross at the bottom, secure with a
piece of floral wire, and wrap with a gold ribbon.

DELAWARE (American holly)
If American holly, Delaware's state tree, is synonymous with Yuletide wreaths, it is partly thanks to such Delaware entrepreneurs as Charlie Jones, the "holly wreath man" of Milton. In 1906, Jones began selling wreaths made of the branches of Delaware's beautiful and plentiful native trees, American holly (*Ilex opaca*), with its serrated leaves and red berries. He shipped holly wreaths across the country in crates labeled FROM THE LAND OF HOLLY. By the thirties, Delaware families were supplementing their winter incomes by gathering American holly in the woods and wiring it to twig-wreath forms made from red-maple branches. The Pennsylvania Railroad had a special route called the Holly Express because it made stops from Delmar, Pennsylvania, to Wilmington, Delaware, for wreath pickups between Thanksgiving and Christmas. By the late forties, plastic wreaths replaced the fresh holly business, and in 1955, the Jones family sold their last wreath, but not before setting the world record at the time for the biggest American holly wreath ever made: It had a diameter of eleven and a half feet and hung at Radio City Music Hall in New York City in 1951.

ABOVE: In November or December, clip 15 branches of holly, each 10" long. Remove the leaves from the lower ends of the stems. Make a wreath form with a 10" diameter by twisting together two freshly cut twigs from a deciduous tree and secure the ends with floral wire. Using a small paintbrush, paint a thin coat of gold luster on all sides of the wreath form, berries, leaves, and twigs. Allow to dry for 3 hours.

RIGHT: Tuck individual branches of holly into the twig base, entwining the branches around the wreath to hold them in place. Secure with 20-gauge brass wire, if needed.

Molded Forms

Molded wreaths are magically light and fun to handle. By far the easiest to make, they are

built on Styrofoam forms or homemade rings cut from corrugated cardboard.

And with a little glue or a few concealed toothpicks, they will support freeze-dried flowers

or fresh cranberries or even an all-American mosaic of dried beans.

MASSACHUSETTS (Cranberries) The tart red fruit that grows wild on Cape Cod and in southeastern Massachusetts was a favorite of the colonists from the moment they tasted it that first Thanksgiving in Plymouth. The pilgrims did not discover the cranberry: Native Americans had long gathered the wild fruit for food and medicinal purposes. The cranberry, dubbed "ruby of the bog" because it grows best in lowland swamps, was so popular that the wild supply was not adequate. Commercial cultivation of this native fruit began in Massachusetts in the 1840s. Today, the state is the nation's top producer of cranberries. Its legislature has even dedicated an official state beverage to accompany the state flower, tree, and coat of arms. That beverage, of course, is cranberry juice.

KANSAS (Sunflowers) In Kansas, the common sunflower grows wild in wheat fields and alongside roads, rotating its head to follow the daily arc of the sun. *Helianthus,* or the wild native sunflower, was declared the state flower in 1903. "This flower has to all Kansans a historic symbolism which speaks of frontier days, winding trails, pathless prairies," the state decreed at the time. Native Americans used and cultivated the sunflower long before Kansas statehood. Archeologists have excavated Indian dwellings from the year 800 and found the charred remains of sunflower seeds. Today, these unpretentious country flowers have become a floral icon, their winsome image turning up on everything from pottery to perfume boxes. It's a trend that might have been predicted by the Kansas legislature of 1903. "Easily sketched, moulded, and carved . . .," said the Kansas Session Laws of the time, "[the sunflower is] ideally adapted for artistic reproduction, with its strong, distinct disk and its golden circle of clear glowing rays." It also happens to be ideally suited to wreath making.

ABOVE: The Massachusetts wreath requires two to three bags of fresh cranberries, two boxes of round toothpicks, and a 14" circular Styrofoam wreath form from a craft store. Round off edges of form with a utility knife. Sort through berries, choosing the largest and hardest fruit. Break toothpicks in half. Stick broken end into berry; push pointed end, with berry attached, into foam. Repeat, placing berries close together. Cover the form, including the edges. Fill any spaces with smaller berries. To protect a wall from staining, pin a red-felt backing, cut to size, on the back of the form. Hang the wreath outside or in a cool room.

OPPOSITE: You'll need about 10 dried sunflower heads, each 4" to 7" wide, to make the Kansas wreath. To make the wreath form, cut corrugated cardboard with a utility knife into a circle 12½" in diameter. Measure another circle 2½" from the outside edge and cut this out, leaving a ring as shown. Use a hot-glue gun to attach sunflower heads to cardboard. Make sure petals overlap slightly so there are no gaps; glue any lost petals into place. To hang, glue a picture-hanger hook onto the back of the wreath form. Don't hang the wreath in direct sun; the petals will fade.

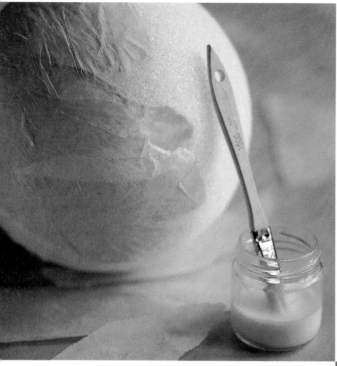

LEFT: The Maryland wreath requires a 10" Styrofoam ball (available at craft stores) and about 70 freeze-dried black-eyed-Susan flower heads (see the Guide). With a screwdriver or a dowel, push a ½"-wide hole through the center of the foam ball. To papier-mâché the foam ball, tear yellow tissue paper into strips. Place these over most of the ball and brush with a mixture of equal parts white glue and water. Let dry, then cover remaining area of ball.

BELOW: Thread a 2'-long piece of twine through the hole; tie a stick to one end so you can hang the ball from the other end while working. Use white glue or a hot-glue gun to attach dried flowers to the ball, overlapping the petals slightly so there are no gaps. Let dry. Measure where you want to hang wreath; add 30". Tie a 2"-wide satin ribbon to twine at top of ball and pull through. Knot ribbon just below the ball, allowing about 18" of ribbon for tail. Hang flowered ball from the ribbon.

MARYLAND (Black-eyed Susans) Even before 1918, when Maryland named the black-eyed Susan its official flower, schoolchildren sang about their native wildflower. "My pretty black-eyed Susan, the prettiest flower that grows," went one such tune, "You're sweeter than sweet violets, the lily, or the rose." Black-eyed Susans (*Rudbeckia hirta),* with their yellow-orange petals and black (really dark-brown) "eyes" shaped like fuzzy cones, spring up wild all over Maryland wherever there is plenty of sun. They flower from mid-June to August, but even when black-eyed Susans are not available, Maryland's residents use a bit of alchemy to create them. Since 1940, the winner of Maryland's famous horse race, the Preakness, has been draped in a blanket of black-eyed Susans instead of the classic roses. But the Preakness is held in May, before the state flower is in bloom. Rather than substitute a less meaningful flower, the solution devised by Maryland florists has been to hand-paint daisies to resemble the black-eyed Susan. Now, every year, two thousand white blooms are dyed so that the Preakness victor can wear a blanket of "black-eyed Susans."

IDAHO (Beans) Idaho is one of the nation's greatest producers of beans, but they are not native to the state. Beans sustained populations from Peru to the American Southwest long before Columbus discovered America. The Spanish conquistadors brought beans back to Europe, and their seeds came to Idaho in the horse-drawn wagons of the state's first settlers. Irrigated by glacial water, bean plants filled the valleys between mountain peaks, nourished by ash-laden soil produced by ancient volcanoes in the region. Today, commercial production of beans in Idaho takes place mainly along the banks of the Snake River, which arches like a smile through the southern part of the state. There, in sun-filled mountain basins with names like Magic and Treasure Valley, nearly 150,000 acres of bean plants are started every May. The tidy rows are then carefully tended until they are ready for harvesting in September. Idaho grows 80 percent of the nation's bean seeds as well as several varieties of edible beans, all high in protein, vitamins, and minerals and low in fat, calories, and sodium. Among them are light and dark red kidney, black, pinto (so named for its mottled seeds), and Great Northern beans. The last variety is a staple of Idaho Bean Soup—as well as Senate Bean Soup, the favorite soup in the United States Senate dining room.

ABOVE: Obtain a pound each of several varieties of Idaho beans, such as pinto, Great Northern, and small white beans. To make the frame, cut 2 pieces of corrugated cardboard with a utility knife into 17"-long oval frames. Glue these frames together (this wreath will need the extra support). Cut out the center so that the ring is 3" wide. Glue beans onto the wreath form in desired pattern, using white craft glue; the Idaho wreath should resemble a braided rug. We alternated the direction the beans were facing in some of the rows; it's easier to glue on the beans across the frame rather than around it. Allow the beans to dry overnight, on a flat surface. To hang the wreath, glue a picture-hanging hook to the back of the cardboard form.

Thatched Forms

Thatched wreaths borrow the technique used to make the roofs of those quintessentially cozy

English cottages. Straw is the traditional thatching material, but many others

can be adapted to the method. These wreaths can be very playful, since the chicken-wire base

can be formed into any shape; one of ours is a tribute to the Liberty Bell.

ABOVE LEFT: The design for the Maine wreath was inspired by the shape of the state flower, the tassel of the Eastern white pine, which appears in clusters on new shoots in the spring. Join 7 white pinecones into a flower shape with floral wire. Use this as a base. Wire or hot-glue 20 more cones around it, forming a sphere.

ABOVE CENTER: The tassel was made by forming a chicken-wire tube with the following measurements: 24" long, 8" wide on the narrow end, 12" on the wide end. (Wear gloves to protect your hands.) Weave floral wire through the seam of the chicken wire, as if sewing the edges together. To create a base from which to hang the tassel, thread a 12"-long stick (1" wide) through the tube's narrow end and secure to tube with floral wire. Attach a 24" piece of floral wire to the center of the stick, as shown. Carefully tie ends around the pinecone sphere (the pinecones are fragile). Twist to secure cones to stick, creating a loop at end.

ABOVE RIGHT: Fill the inside of the chicken wire with 3' branches of pine, wiring branches to stick (this will help the tassel keep its shape). Thatch smaller branches of pine to the outside of the chicken wire by weaving stems through holes in chicken wire. Start at the bottom of the tassel, overlapping layers until you reach the top. Wrap tassel with green floral wire, and knot the wire at the end. Hide wire by "fluffing" up the pine needles. Trim the bottom of the tassel to even it off, and clip ends of the stick, if they're visible. Hang from the loop.

MAINE (Eastern white pine) With its towering height and trunk as straight as a pole, there is no mistaking Eastern white pine, the tallest conifer in the Northeast. Eastern white pine is the official tree of Maine, the Pine Tree State; its pinecone and tassel (the small yellow flower that appears on new shoots) are the state's floral emblem. This native evergreen, which grows up to one hundred feet tall, once grew so densely in the northeastern United States that, according to legend, a squirrel could live its entire life without ever coming down from the pines. Native Americans gathered its bark for medicine, and the colonists used its high-quality wood to build houses and churches. The trunk was valued for ship masts during the colonial period; Maine's early settlers were upset when the British took the tallest trees to build the Royal Navy. Today, Eastern white pine grows across Maine, and you can hear "the wind blowing through the pines" throughout the state, says George Bourassa, a forester with the Maine Forest Service. "It is a sound you never forget," he says.

PENNSYLVANIA (Mountain laurel)
Pennsylvania's wreath form was
designed to resemble the state's best-
known icon, the Liberty Bell, which rang
out on July 8, 1776, to announce the
first public reading of the Declaration
of Independence. When the bell was
ordered cast in 1751 for the Pennsylvania
State House, the Speaker of the
Assembly had it inscribed with a verse
from Leviticus, saying "Proclaim liberty
throughout all the land unto all the
inhabitants thereof." He was acknowl-
edging Pennsylvania's history of
religious liberty, a right the colonists
had been guaranteed by their founder,
William Penn. The bell rang for public
announcements many times before
1776, but it only became known as
the Liberty Bell after the War of
Independence. It has remained dear
to Pennsylvania's residents as well as
to all Americans. A million and a half
people visit Independence Hall in
downtown Philadelphia every year to
see the bell and the place where
freedom rang. Our thatched bell was
made of mountain-laurel leaves,
Pennsylvania's state flower, which
produces spectacular cup-shaped
flowers in the spring. But it could be
made of any other evergreen material
for celebrations of Independence
Day in your state.

ABOVE: Begin making the Pennsylvania wreath by shaping chick-
en wire into the form of a bell, wearing gloves to protect your
hands. Cut the wire into a rectangle 12" wide and 47" long. Bend
the rectangle into a long tube, and crimp the long ends to close
seam. To shape the tube into a bell, squeeze tube in the middle to
make an hourglass shape, as shown in the photograph. Cut out a
12"-round piece of chicken wire and place it like a cap on top of
the hourglass, pressing the structure into a bell shape. Bend the
edges to fasten the seam. Trim off any uneven edges with scissors.

OPPOSITE: Cut about 100 branches of mountain laurel into 6"-
long branch tips. Strip the leaves off the bottom of each branch
tip, leaving 3" of stem visible. Starting at the bottom of the bell,
weave stripped ends of branch tips through the chicken wire,
working around the bell. Thatch the entire bell form in this
manner, overlapping the previous layer by half. To make the
bell's clapper, hang a silver or glass ornament from a wire
attached to the inside top of the bell form. Hang wreath from a
ribbon threaded through the top of the bell form.

NEW JERSEY (Boxwood) Since the villas of ancient Rome, boxwood has been a favored garden plant for edging flower beds and forming hedges, as well as for topiary work. The boxwood shrub, also known as box, has small, glossy green leaves that are easily manicured. In the United States, the evergreen boxwood (*Buxus*) has long been a staple of historic gardens such as the Duke Estate in Somerville, New Jersey. This classic garden plant is therefore a fitting material for a wreath in honor of the Garden State. That official nickname originated with the small New Jersey truck farms that once supplied fruit and vegetables to the nearby urban centers of New York and Philadelphia. New Jersey's vegetable crops, especially tomatoes, are still important to the state, but they have been surpassed in economic importance by another growing agricultural business: the nurseries concentrated in central and southern New Jersey that sell perennials, herbs, and, naturally, boxwood. These nurseries supply gardens all over the country, making New Jersey's nickname more apt than ever today.

ABOVE: For the New Jersey wreath you'll need to cut four 3'-by-2' strips of chicken wire. Arrange in a square and place a 3'-square wire-wreath frame (see the Guide) over them. Cover the frame with sphagnum moss. Wearing work gloves to protect your hands, fold each side of chicken wire over moss and frame, and bind the seam by weaving floral wire through the chicken wire. Moisten the moss.

RIGHT: Clip the tips of 75 bushy boxwood branches into 6" long pieces. Strip the bottom 3" of leaves from each piece. Weave the stems into the chicken wire, overlapping previous tips by half. Thatch boxwood in the same direction on one side; alternate the direction on remaining sides. Cut floral wire into 2" pieces and bend into U shapes, and use these as reinforcements. When all sides are complete, trim the boxwood. Attach 2 wire loops to the back of the wreath, thread a ribbon through loops, and hang.

OKLAHOMA
WINTER WHEAT

Gathered Wreaths

Some crops are more than just a symbol of the state. The wheat fields of Oklahoma, the vast

woods of Michigan, the sweet prairies of Illinois live in the consciousness of

their residents. This chapter presents a variety of techniques designed to show off a single

material in the most dramatic—and occasionally poignant—way.

ABOVE: Oklahoma's gathered wreath was made of golden winter wheat. Assemble 200 stalks of wheat. To heighten their natural color, we spray-painted the stalks with two coats of gold paint, but they would look just as beautiful if the wheat were left natural. Let the paint dry for a day. Bunch the wheat together, and tie with a 4" wide ribbon.

LEFT: To make the South Carolina wreath, gather about 50 okra pods, each 6" to 8" long, with 2" of stem attached (see the Guide). Lay the pods on a screen to dry in a very hot, dry place—an attic is ideal. The sides will split as they dry (about three weeks), producing a striped effect. When the pods are ready (choose the 36 that looked the nicest), you will need about 100 yards of raffia. Tie 3 strands of raffia 2' to 3' long to each okra stem.

BELOW RIGHT: Take 3 okra pods with raffia attached, and braid together for 2" starting from the stem, as pictured at left. Repeat for remaining pods. Braid 2 of these clusters together for 2". Braid in another okra cluster, overlapping the previous group by half. Continue braiding in clusters until all the okra pods have been incorporated. Make a thick braid with the remaining raffia, and tie in a knot to hang.

OKLAHOMA (Winter wheat) The title song from the Rodgers and Hammerstein musical *Oklahoma!* is buried so deep in the American psyche that probably no one can say the name of the state without humming to themselves that, "The wavin' wheat can sure smell sweet when the wind comes right behind the rain." The wheat that's so identified with the state came to the Great Plains in the last century via Mennonite immigrants from the Ukraine. They sewed the seeds of the hard bread wheat variety known as Hard Red Winter Wheat into the hems and cuffs of their dresses. "Our climate was very similar to theirs, so it did very well here," says Mike Frickenschmidt, an Oklahoma wheat farmer and a descendent of German pioneers. Today, he says, "a lot of the gals do wheat weaving. I've seen the shape of the State of Oklahoma done in wheat down at the State Capitol."

SOUTH CAROLINA (Okra)
Legend has it that okra was brought to the New World from Africa by slaves who hid its seeds in their hair. However it made its way here, it would be hard to imagine American southern cuisine without okra. South Carolinians eat okra's hexagonal pods raw with salt and pepper, fried in batter, pickled, and stewed in gumbo. While okra is no longer grown commercially in South Carolina, many residents of the state still cultivate it in their gardens—a labor of love, since okra's prickly pods are notoriously itchy. There is a payoff: Okra (*Abelmoschus esculentus)*, a cousin of hibiscus, produces lovely yellow flowers from the beginning of July until the first frost. "When you see thousands of those things in flower," says Dr. Roy Ogle, a professor emeritus of horticulture at Clemson University in South Carolina, "they are spectacular."

BELOW: The Michigan wreath is made with fall-foliage branches such as maple and oak, with leaves attached, as well as acorns and pressed ferns. Let leaves dry on the branches; let acorns dry until they turn brown. Attach leaves and ferns to twigs by wrapping stems together with brown floral tape. To prepare the acorns, remove their caps, then reattach with wood glue so they don't fall off once wreath is assembled. Glue a 6" piece of floral wire to the stub of an acorn cap. Let dry, then cover wire with floral tape. Attach acorns to oak branches with floral tape; position acorns by bending floral wire as desired. Arrange the branches, leaves, and ferns on a flat surface to find an arrangement that pleases you, then gather the stems together, secure with wire, and cover with a wide ribbon.

MICHIGAN (Woodland) Few states have as much forest as Michigan, where more than half the total landmass is wooded. Michigan's fall-foliage season is one of the most spectacular in the country, and people follow the changing of the leaves south, from the Upper Peninsula to the Lower. "It looks as if a painter had spilled paint on his or her palette," says Tom Woiwode, director of the Michigan chapter of the Nature Conservancy. "The colors just run over." Most of Michigan's original forest cover was lost in the nineteenth century to logging, fire, and land clearing by farmers. Fortunately, in this century, Michigan has taken great care to heal and rebuild its forests. Much of its woodlands are now maturing into the growth phase known as "climax forest," which consists of a mixture of trees young and old, including valuable timber trees such as white pine, yellow birch, and sugar maple. The timber industry continues to be important in Michigan, but there are limits on the number of trees that can be cut down each year. As a result, the forest is rapidly expanding.

NEVADA (Tumbleweed) In the movies, tumbleweed has always evoked the Old West, where massive balls of twisted gray branches bounce past campfires and cling like burrs to barbed-wire fences. "You could make a twenty-foot wreath just by going out on a windy day and letting them blow into the car," said Dr. Teri Knight, a Nevada botanist, when we proposed using tumbleweed, also known as Russian thistle (*Salsola kali),* to symbolize her state. Although it is hard to imagine the Nevada desert without it, tumbleweed did not exist in the United States until the mid nineteenth century. Its seeds were embedded in the fur and hooves of pack animals that immigrants brought from Europe to America on ships. The Russian-thistle seeds promptly got stuck in mud that was in turn spread all over Nevada on the wooden wheels of wagon trains going west. Now, tumbleweeds germinate all over the western United States. Each plant sprouts upright shoots, which grow leaves in February, stay rooted for a couple of months, and then dry out, forming a birdcage shape, often four-by-five-feet wide and high, that is swept away by the desert wind. "On a great windstorm afternoon in summer," Dr. Knight says, "you'll see hundreds of these tumbling beachballs blowing by."

ABOVE: We wired a single tumbleweed with white lights and hung it to create a chandelier effect with the Nevada wreath. You'll need a tumbleweed and a string of 100 tiny white lights attached to an extension cord. Wearing gloves and a long-sleeved shirt to protect your hands and forearms, push the cord of lights through the stem end of the tumbleweed. Cut a notch in one end of a stick and use it to push the lights deeper into the middle of the brush. The cord and plug should hang outside at the top. With the stick, push lights so they appear uniformly through the tumbleweed. Hide the plug where the lights meet the extension cord by pushing it into the tumbleweed and securing with wire. Twine can be coiled around the exposed cord wire to cover. Suspend the tumbleweed—and plug it in.

OREGON (Apples and pears) Oregon's Hood River Valley, near the border with Washington, sits in the middle of a ring of fire. The valley is surrounded by volcanic mountains and has the perfect growing conditions for apples and pears, with rich volcanic soil, warm days, cool nights, and plenty of moisture. Apple and pear trees grow from the valley floor right up to the foot of the mountains, and in April, the entire basin is scented with the smell of their white and red blossoms. Such growing conditions have made Oregon one of the top orchard states in the nation. There are two main orchard areas in Oregon. The Hood River Valley specializes in the green-skinned Anjou pears, which are juicy and spicy-sweet. The Rogue River Valley, north of the California border, grows such pears as Bosc, Bartlett, Comice, and red-skinned varieties. Apples of all sorts grow in both mountain basins (as does asparagus, which grows like a weed in Oregon's orchards, having escaped from old farms nearby). Oregon has taken great pains with its pear industry, an accomplishment given the patience necessary to cultivate this delicate fruit. Pear trees take up to nine years to bear fruit, and when they do, the pears must be picked by hand. As the old saying goes, "Plant pears for your heirs."

ABOVE: The Oregon wreath requires about 40 apples, 12 pears, and a special straight-wire form (see the Guide). Cut a square of transparent material such as iridescent stocking or, as shown here, antique gold-mesh ribbon large enough to wrap around each fruit. Tie off with a 12"-long piece of 22-gauge brass wire.

OPPOSITE: Gather 3 wrapped fruits and twist their wires together. Starting at the lowest rung on the straight-wire form, hang a group of 3 by wrapping their wires around the form. At the next rung, attach a second bunch of fruit, leaving wires long enough so the fruit hang just above the previous bunch. Attach another group of fruit to the same rung, but shorten wires so they hang higher. Stagger the fruit evenly along the frame. Continue until the entire frame is covered with fruit, with no visible gaps. Tuck leaves between fruits for added decoration and to hide any gaps. Attach a loop of wire to the penultimate rung, then hang. Thread ribbon through top rung; loop around wire and notch ends.

OHIO
OHIO BUCKEYE

ILLINOIS
PRAIRIE GRASS

LEFT: Collect about 75 Ohio-buckeye nuts. You'll also need 20-gauge brass wire and 75 brass beads. Use a Dremel drill with a $^1/_{16}$" bit to make a hole through the "eye" of each buckeye. Cut brass wire into 22"-long pieces, thread on a bead, and fold wire in half. The bead should be at the fold. Push the ends of the folded wire through the hole in the buckeye, so the bead is in the center of the eye. With a needle-nose plier, twist wire tightly, as shown, leaving wire ends loose. Repeat with all the buckeyes.

BELOW RIGHT: Take 3 buckeyes and twist their wires together. Make 2 more clusters. Twist these clusters together. Create several groups of 4 buckeyes, and attach these by wiring above the first group. Keep making and adding clusters of 4 buckeyes until you've created a shape similar to a cluster of grapes. The widest part—at the top—should have clusters of 5 buckeyes each. Twist remaining wire into a loop. Tie a gold ribbon to the wire to cover it. Knot the ribbon, creating a loop, and hang. Cut ends and style so they resemble leaves.

OHIO (Ohio buckeye) Ohioans are not shy about their fondness for their state tree, Ohio buckeye (*Aesculus glabra*), which gets its name from the resemblance of its nut to the eye of the white-tailed buck. Ohio's nickname is the Buckeye State. Ohio State University's top-ranked sports teams are called the Buckeyes. What's more, the term "buckeye" is pretty much synonymous with "I'm from Ohio." The buckeye grows wild along streams and rivers in the state, climbing to an average height of sixty feet (the national champion is one hundred and sixteen feet high). Its shiny-brown nut, which falls to the forest floor in autumn, is not edible. Before the Civil War, the word buckeye was used as a synonym for "worthless" because the wood of its tree was weak. That usage disappeared when William Henry Harrison, who carried a buckeye walking stick, became the first Ohioan president of the United States in 1841. Buckeye nuts are considered lucky; many Ohio fans carry them in their pockets at football games–which might help to explain OSU's perennial success.

ILLINOIS (Prairie grass) Once, much of Illinois was covered with tallgrass prairie, a broad expanse of native grass so high you had to stand up in the saddle in order to spot the grazing cattle. The grass had names like Big Bluestem, Prairie Dropseed, and the sweet-smelling Vanilla Grass. In early accounts, some pioneers said traveling through the prairie grass, all uniform in height, its overall surface undulating infinitely toward the horizon, felt like being adrift at sea. Then came the sod busters, strong young men whose job it was to break the notoriously dense prairie sod for the pioneers, a task they accomplished with a team of eight oxen pulling an enormous iron plow. The prairie disappeared rapidly after John Deere invented the steel plow in 1837, but in the past twenty years, Illinois conservationists have spurred projects to restore the state's tallgrass prairie. These include the Nachusa Grasslands in northern Illinois as well as the Midewin National Tallgrass Prairie forty-five miles southwest of Chicago.

ABOVE: The Illinois wreath can be made out of any tall prairie grass, such as Little Bluestem or switchgrass (we used the latter). Both are available fresh at many plant nurseries in Illinois. To make the wreath, gather a bunch of fresh tall prairie grass. Take a smaller bunch of prairie grass and cut off the tops so only the stems remain. Place under the larger bunch, cross over in front, and secure the ends in back with hot glue. If you're using dried prairie grass, secure the bunch with floral wire, and cover the wire with a ribbon or bow.

The United States of America

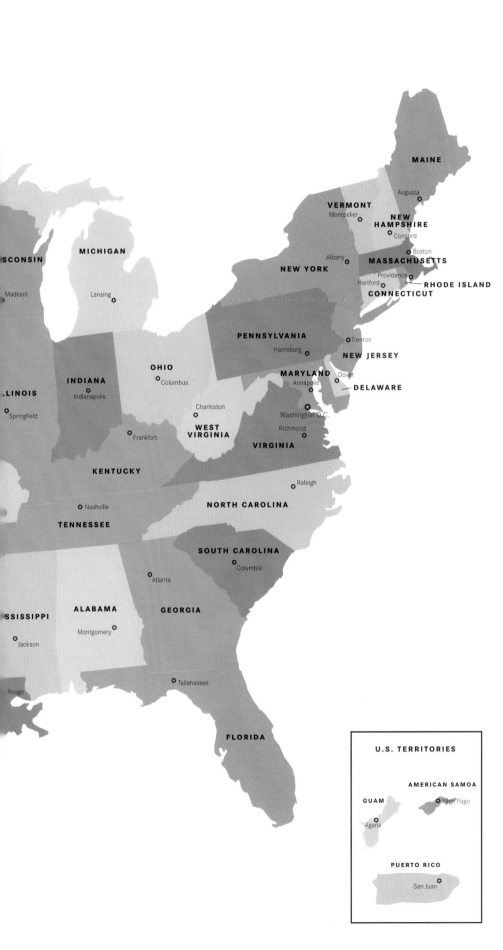

ALABAMA cotton

ALASKA sitka spruce

ARIZONA cactus

ARKANSAS rice

CALIFORNIA rosemary and olive branches

COLORADO blue spruce

CONNECTICUT mountain laurel

DELAWARE American holly

FLORIDA citrus fruits

GEORGIA pecans

HAWAII orchids

IDAHO beans

ILLINOIS prairie grass

INDIANA peonies

IOWA dent corn

KANSAS sunflowers

KENTUCKY bluegrass

LOUISIANA magnolia

MAINE eastern white pine

MARYLAND black-eyed Susans

MASSACHUSETTS cranberries

MICHIGAN woodland

MINNESOTA red Norway pine

MISSISSIPPI magnolias

MISSOURI black walnuts

MONTANA ponderosa pinecones

NEBRASKA miniature Indian corn

NEVADA tumbleweed

NEW HAMPSHIRE pussy-willow

NEW JERSEY boxwood

NEW MEXICO sagebrush

NEW YORK rose hips

NORTH CAROLINA fraser fir

NORTH DAKOTA oats and barley

OHIO Ohio buckeye

OKLAHOMA winter wheat

OREGON apples and pears

PENNSYLVANIA mountain laurel

RHODE ISLAND quahaug shells

SOUTH CAROLINA okra

SOUTH DAKOTA hay

TENNESSEE galax

TEXAS yellow roses

U.S. TERRITORIES tropical leaves

UTAH mixed evergreens

VIRGINIA dogwood

VERMONT sugar-maple leaves

WASHINGTON moss

WASHINGTON, D.C. white oak

WEST VIRGINIA rhododendron

WISCONSIN wood violets

WYOMING limber pine

Acknowledgments and Credits

Special thanks to the staff of MARTHA STEWART LIVING
and the following people for sharing their time and knowledge:

GENERAL ASSISTANCE

The National Parks Service; the United States Department of Agriculture; the USDA Forest Service;
and universities, agricultural boards, and park and forestry services in every state

STYLING AND LOCATION ASSISTANCE

Page Marchese, Shannon Goodson, Jerry Bolduan of Green Valley Growers, Kevin Burger,
Louis DeRienzo, Jeff Allen, Cory Tippen, Julie Flynn, Laura Sewrey, Anne Johnson,
Brian Milman, Lois Milman, Suzie Flax, Ken Crivello, Don P. Marchese, Beth Gill of Aspen Branch Floral Arts,
Brian Lovett, Mike Cuhns of Utah State University, Libbie and Bo Dougan, Cheryl Amestoy,
Kenneth and Shirley Bloomer, Richard Hampton Jenrette, Dr. Gerald Imber

ADMINISTRATION

David Steward, Sharon Patrick, Shelley Lewis Waln

EDITORIAL

Stephen Drucker, Melissa Morgan, Margaret Roach, Molly Tully

PHOTO EDITING

Heidi Posner, Kevin Guterl

RESEARCH

Heidi K. Petelinz, Julia Loktev, Matthew Benson, Diana Jeffrey, Rachel Coleman

EDITORIAL PRODUCTION

Marcel Sarmiento, Tiffany Wardle

PUBLISHING

Lauren Podlach Stanich, Rich Fontaine, Alisa Kigner

PRODUCTION

Dora Braschi Cardinale, George D. Planding, Nicole M. Lobisco

COLOR SEPARATIONS

Ernest V. Cardinale of Satellite Graphics

PRINTING

Quebecor Printing, Kingsport, Tennessee

Guide

Addresses and telephone numbers of sources are correct as of August 1996
but are subject to change, as are the price and availability of any item.

COVER

Martha Stewart walking with the sugar-maple-leaf wreath of Vermont. Hermés women's QUILTED JACKET at Hermés stores nationwide. Call 800-441-4488 for store information. Blue SHIRT by J.Crew. HAIR AND MAKEUP by Brett Jackson for Sarah Laird. FASHION STYLING by Darcy Miller.

INTRODUCTION

To make the Washington, D.C., wreath, you'll need a 36" straw form (see page 50) wrapped with gold ribbon, 180 oak leaves, and 90 acorns, both with stems attached. Dry and gild acorns as described on page 100. Press leaves overnight between two heavy books. Spray paint leaves with gold paint. Tape a 9" piece of floral wire to each leaf stem, covering length of wire with floral tape. Glue a 5" piece of floral wire to the stub of each acorn cap. Let dry, then cover wire with floral tape. To assemble wreath, gather acorns in groups of 3 and tape stems together; tape the leaves together in groups of 6. Fan out the groups. Attach to wreath with floral pins, overlapping previous groups by half.

**GENERAL WREATH
MAKING SUPPLIES**

22-gauge GREEN FLORAL WIRE on a paddle, $1.60 for 114 feet; FLORAL TAPE, $1.70 per roll; and 1©" steel FLORAL PINS, $1 for 60, all from Dorothy Biddle Service, HC 01, Box 900, Greeley, PA 18425; 717-226-3239. Assorted natural, wire, and synthetic WREATH FORMS, and TINY WHITE LIGHTS, all from Joe Makrancy's Garden and Floral Shop, 966 Kuser Road, Trenton, NJ 08619; 609-587-2543. SQUARE, ROUND, and CUSTOM WIRE-WREATH FORMS, all from Galveston Wreath Company, 1124 25th Street, Galveston, TX 77550-4409; 409-765-8597. Free catalog. ASSORTED EVERGREEN BRANCHES, $1 per pound, from Oregon Roses, Inc., 1170 East Tualatin Valley Highway, Hillsboro, OR 97123; 503-648-8551. RIBBONS from Hyman Hendler & Sons, 67 West 38th Street, New York, NY 10018; 212-840-8393. VINTAGE RIBBONS from Bell'occhio, 8 Brady Street, San Francisco, CA 94103; 415-864-4048. ASSORTED RIBBONS by C.M. Offray & Son at ribbon and notions stores nation-wide. DREMEL MULTI-PRO DRILL and D-VICE, from Dremel, 4915 21st Street, Racine, WI 53406; 800-437-3635.

Free catalog. 4-mm solid BRASS BEADS, $8.50 for 100 beads; BRASS WIRE: $9.50 per pound for 8-gauge; $6 per pound for 18-gauge; $8.75 per pound for 20-gauge; and $11.20 per pound for 24-gauge, all from Metalliferous, 34 West 46th Street, New York, NY 10036; 212-944-0909. RAFFIA from Knud Nielsen. Call 800-698-5656 for nearest distributor. GOLD SPRAY PAINT available at art-supply stores nationwide. 20-gauge COPPER WIRE, $3 per 6-meter roll, and FISHING LINE, 71¢ for 50 yards, both from Pearl Paint, 308 Canal Street, New York, NY 10013; 212-431-7932 or 800-221-6845. CHICKEN WIRE available at hardware stores nationwide.

WIRE WREATHS

pages 16, 19
MAGNOLIA LEAVES, $16 per bunch, from Green Valley Growers, 10450 Cherry Ridge Road, Sebastopol, CA 95472; 707-823-5583.

pages 22, 24
FRASER FIR, $20 for 15- to 20-pound box, from Bald Mountain Farm, P.O. Box 138, Todd, NC 28684; 910-385-6419 or 800-577-9622.

pages 23, 25

PUSSY WILLOW at florists nationwide.

pages 36, 38

SNOWFLAKE WREATH FORM, $25, from Martha By Mail, 800-950-7130. SITKA SPRUCE and DOUGLAS FIR BRANCHES, $1 per pound, from Oregon Roses, Inc., 1170 East Tualatin Valley Highway, Hillsboro, OR 97123; 503-648-8551.

pages 37, 39

FREEZE-DRIED YELLOW ROSES, $1.50 per flower, from O.K.S. Flowers, Inc., 123 West 28th Street, New York, NY 10001; 212-268-7231.

pages 40, 42

ORCHIDS, $5 to $15 per spray, from Santa Barbara Gardens and Company, P.O. Box 6701, Santa Barbara, CA 93111; 805-967-5049. Also available from Na Pua O Maui Florist, 1215 South Kihei Road, Kihei, Maui, HI 96753; 808-879-0696. PLASTIC FLOWER VIALS, $14.95 for 100, from Kervar, Inc., 119-121 West 28th Street, New York, NY 10001; 212-564-2525.

pages 41, 43

TROPICAL LEAVES from Na Pua O Maui Florist, see above.

pages 44, 46

RICE available seasonally from Terry Farm Partnership, 4305 Dick Jeter Road, North Little Rock, AK 72117; 501-945-5115.

pages 45, 47

COTTON, $8 per bunch, from O.K.S. Flowers, Inc., see above.

STRAW FORMS

pages 48, 49, 51

MOUNTAIN LAUREL, $16 per bunch, from Green Valley Growers, 10450 Cherry Ridge Road, Sebastopol, CA 95472; 707-823-5583.

pages 52, 53

FREEZE-DRIED PEONIES, $6 per head, from Plan Decor, 980 David Road, Suite E, Burlingame, CA 94010; 415-548-9004. Free catalog. Also available from O.K.S. Flowers, Inc., 123 West 28th Street, New York, NY 10001; 212-268-7231.

LIVING WREATHS

pages 58 to 65

18" LIVING-WREATH FORM, $60 with moss, from Teddy Colbert's Garden, P.O. Box 9, Somis, CA 93066; 800-833-3981.

RECOMMENDED READING: *The Living Wreath,* by Teddy Colbert (Gibbs-Smith Publisher, 1996; $19.95).

page 61

ASSORTED MOSSES available from Fertile Ground, 33335 SE Regan Hill Road, Estacada, OR 97023; 503-630-7723.

pages 62, 64

WOOD VIOLETS, $2.60 per plant, from Gardens of the Blue Ridge, P.O. Box 10, Pineola, NC 28662; 704-733-2417. Catalog $3.

pages 63, 65

BLUEGRASS SOD from Pacific Sod, 305 Hueneme Road, Camarillo, CA 93012; 805-986-8279 or 800-942-5296. California orders only. BLUEGRASS SEED available from nurseries wherever bluegrass grows.

SWAGS AND GARLANDS

pages 66, 68

GALAX at florists nationwide.

pages 67, 69, 70

MAGNOLIA LEAVES, $16 per bunch, available from Green Valley Growers, 10450 Cherry Ridge Road, Sebastopol, CA 95472; 707-823-5583.

pages 71 to 73

BARLEY (and other grains) available from Knud Nielsen. Call 800-698-5656 for more information.

pages 74, 75

INDIAN CORN, $2 for 3 ears, available from Windy Maple Farms, RD#10, Box 112, Middletown, NY 10940; 914-342-2648. Pretty Pops ORNAMENTAL MINI INDIAN CORN, $9.50 for 25 ears or $37 per case of 100, available from Eckler's Produce & Greenhouse, 1879 Barron Lake Road, Niles, MI 49120-9368; 616-683-2509.

pages 76, 79, 81

BLACK WALNUTS, $7.65 per pound, available from Missouri Dandy Pantry, 414 North Street, Stockton, MO 65785; 800-872-6879. Free catalog.

TWIG WREATHS

pages 82, 84

ROSE-HIP BRANCHES available at florists nationwide.

pages 83, 85

PRESSED DOGWOOD BLOSSOMS available from Knud Nielsen. Call 800-698-5656 for more information.

pages 87 to 89

FRUITED OLIVE BRANCHES, $18 per bunch, and FLOWERING ROSEMARY, $12 per bunch, available seasonally from Green Valley Growers, 10450 Cherry Ridge Road, Sebastopol, CA 95472; 707-823-5583. GRAPEVINE BRANCHES from Joe Makrancy's Garden and Floral Shop, 966 Kuser Road, Trenton, NJ 08619; 609-587-2543.

pages 90, 92, 93

PINE BRANCHES available at local nurseries and garden centers.

pages 91, 94, 95

RHODODENDRON BRANCHES can be ordered from your local florist.

pages 96, 97

PINE BRANCHES available at local nurseries and garden centers.

pages 98, 100

22-karat Italian GOLD LEAF, $24.50 for 25 sheets, from Pearl Paint, 308 Canal Street, New York, NY 10013; 212-431-7932 or 800-221-6845.

pages 99, 101

LIQUID LEAF PAINT in Classic Gold (#6110), $3.18 for .75-ounce jar, from Pearl Paint, see above.

MODELED FORMS

pages 102, 104

SUNFLOWERS from Knud Nielsen. Call 800-698-5656 for more information.

pages 103, 105

FRESH CRANBERRY WREATH, $100, from Maurice Parkonen, Jr., Carver Road, West Wareham, MA 02576; 508-295-2558. Paradise Meadow brand FRESH CRANBERRIES, from Decas Cranberry Company, available nationwide.

pages 106, 108

DRIED BLACK-EYED SUSANS from Knud Nielsen. see above. 8" STYRO-FOAM BALLS at craft stores nationwide.

page 107, 109

Assorted DRIED BEANS available at supermarkets nationwide.

THATCHED FORMS

pages 110, 112, 113

WHITE-PINE BRANCHES, PINE-CONES, and OTHER EVERGREENS at local nurseries and garden centers. ASSORTED EVERGREENS available from Oregon Roses, Inc., 1170 East Tualatin Valley Highway, Hillsboro, OR 97123; 503-648-8551.

pages 111, 115

MOUNTAIN LAUREL, $16 per bunch, from Green Valley Growers, 10450 Cherry Ridge Road, Sebastopol, CA 95472; 707-823-5583.

pages 116, 117

BOXWOOD, $16 per bunch, from Green Valley Growers, 10450 Cherry Ridge Road, Sebastopol, CA 95472; 707-823-5583.

GATHERED WREATHS

pages 118, 120, 121

WHEAT SHEAVES, $15 per bunch, available from Lynn Carmichael, Country Wheat Weaving, 6109 Quail Lane, Enid, OK 73703; 405-233-5040. Also available from Knud Nielsen. Call 800-698-5656 for more information.

pages 119, 121

OKRA, $6 for 18 pods, from Green Valley Growers, see above.

pages 127 to 129

STRAIGHT METAL WREATH FRAME, $4 for 2' frame, available from Joe Makrancy's Garden and Floral Shop, 966 Kuser Road, Trenton, NJ 08619; 609-587-2543. Also from Galveston Wreath Company, 1124 25th Street, Galveston, TX 77550-4409; 409-765-8597. Free catalog.

pages 131, 133

ORNAMENTAL and NATIVE PRAIRIE GRASSES available seasonally from the Natural Garden, 38 West 443, Highway 64, St. Charles, IL 60175; 630-584-0150. PRAIRIE-GRASS SEEDS, $2 to $15 per ½-ounce package, available from Prairie Nursery, P.O. Box 306, Westfield, WI 53964; 608-296-3679.

HOW TO TIE A BOW

Many of the wreaths in this book can be finished off with a large, lavish bow.
A crisp ribbon (grosgrain, satin, taffeta, or velvet are ideal fabrics) will make the nicest bow.
Attach the ribbon to the wreath with a small piece of green florist's wire.

1 Cut the ribbon to desired length.
(A bow with extra-large loops or extra-long tails will need more length.) Form into two equal loops with about twelve inches of ribbon between them.

2 Cross the right loop over the left.

3 Knot the loops by pushing the right loop behind the left, under, and through the hole.

4 Pull knot tight; adjust loops and tails to desired size. Lightly fold the ends and cut, creating a notch.

5 The finished bow, ready to be attached.

Index BY MATERIALS

Index BY STATE